The Art of Solving Problems

The Art of
Solving Problems

●●●●●●

K. F. JACKSON

HEINEMANN : LONDON

William Heinemann Ltd
15 Queen St, Mayfair, London W1X 8BE

LONDON MELBOURNE TORONTO
JOHANNESBURG AUCKLAND

To Pat, Elizabeth, and Andrew

Printed by Morrison & Gibb Ltd
London and Edinburgh

Contents

v

Preface

An experience of twenty years ago was the origin of the train of events which led to the writing of this book. It was one of those turning points in life of the kind where the realization that something is unsatisfactory suddenly becomes an awareness of opportunities for improvement. In some research work I was doing I had recorded a quantity of results and found that I had little idea how to get useful information out of them. When I realized how unsatisfactory and wasteful this state of affairs was, I became acutely conscious of the need for careful planning, not only in research but in all kinds of activities and occupations. This experience set me on a search for a systematic method of planning, and when I had found out something about it I was able to make considerable improvements in my methods of working and was encouraged to pass these ideas on to others.

Later on, I made some more discoveries. I began to realize that planning was not the whole of what I had been seeking. It became apparent that although planning is a valuable technique for many purposes, these purposes are not achievable by planning alone. At this stage I became aware of the importance of problems. In a sense, problems are the stuff of which all work and human endeavour is composed. The techniques I had been looking for were really the methods of problem-solving, of which planning is one among many. I then found out for the first time about the literature of problem-solving and its component topics such as decision-making and creativity. I learnt that this literature originated in ancient times and after centuries of fits and starts had entered a period of rapid growth during the same period as my own investigations.

Problem-solving methods have the useful property of being applicable to themselves. It was natural that I should use them to identify steps in the problem-solving process for which I could not find ready-made methods of attack and to devise further material to fill the gaps.

As I developed my knowledge of the subject I was at the same time developing methods of teaching problem-solving to managers. It was the request of students on one of the early courses to be given more to read which caused me to think seriously about writing this book. The preparation and conduct of courses and the writing of the book have contributed much to my understanding of the subject and I am very grateful to my students for encouragement and many useful ideas, comments, and practical examples.

Although many of the examples have been taken from business life, the book has been written primarily for the general reader and the student. It is only the chapters on implementation which have greater relevance to management.

In putting the book together I have attempted to provide a logical explanation of the nature of problems and to give practical advice on how to tackle every stage of solving them. I believe that some of this material is original, although much is well known and can be found in other books. Parts of what I have written may appear to be rather obvious, but I trust it will be appreciated that some things need to be said for the sake of completeness, and in any case what is obvious to some people is not obvious to others. My justification for producing another book in this field is that there are few which set out to explain a comprehensive set of general and practical methods for problem-solving. The small number of really practical books, some of which are mentioned in a list at the end of this one, tend to cover special topics or special fields of application.

The purpose of writing this book is not to propound either a logical theory or a psychological theory of problem-solving but to give practical advice. It is not a book about how problem-solving could be done or is done, but how it can be done more effectively. The emphasis is very much on the doing, because it is not sufficient to know how to solve problems, it is necessary to acquire better habits of thinking and working if we are to make any substantial improvement in our ability to solve them. I have included many practical exercises to encourage readers to make a serious attempt to carry out the advice given in the text. I would not advise you to regard them in the same way as a course of physical exercises to be pursued slavishly, but rather as an opportunity to try out the methods described in the text and to test your own skills. Another way to look upon them is as a source of clues to help you find ways of tackling your own problems, both now and in the future. There is no reason why you should not start with the exercises which appear to be more interesting or relevant to your needs, and try the others later on, when you have acquired greater understanding and skill and confidence in the use of problem-solving methods.

In order to minimize problems in communication I have tried to avoid scientific and technical language, and to help identify myself with readers I have frequently referred to myself and them together as 'we'. When speaking of a particular sort of person or a person in particular circumstances I have generally used 'he' in preference to 'he or she', not in order to exclude the feminine but for the sake of simplicity and clarity.

I wish readers every success in their study of this subject and hope that in reading this book they will experience some of the pleasure that I have had in the writing.

K. F. JACKSON

Gerrards Cross, Bucks

Acknowledgments

I am grateful to the British Oxygen Company and Pergamon Press for permission to quote from the article on 'Method Change at BOC'; the McGraw-Hill Book Company for permission to quote from the headings of the principles of searching from *An Introduction to Scientific Research*, by E. Bright Wilson; The Laird Group for permission to quote from an advertisement in *The Times*; Her Majesty's Stationery Office for permission to quote from the *Report of the Committee of Inquiry on Decimal Currency*, Cmnd. 2145, and the *First Report of the Royal Commission on Environmental Pollution*, Cmnd. 4585; Professor Alec Rodger and the National Institute of Industrial Psychology for permission to quote the headings of the *Seven Point Plan*.

I have tried to give credit for ideas gathered from other authors by mentioning them in the text, and if I have failed to do so adequately in any instance I hope that this will not cause offence.

My greatest thanks go to my wife Pat for helping me to make the original decision to write this book, for support and encouragement during the several years that the work has taken, and for reading the manuscript. Barbara McWalter typed the final draft for publication.

I also wish to thank a very large number of friends, relations, and colleagues who have contributed to my collection of examples of real problem-situations, either by telling me about their own problems or just by being themselves and playing their part in situations that created problems for me.

K. F. J.

INTRODUCTION

I

The Nature and Origins
of Problems

May I ask you some questions?

What is your objective in reading this book? Did you pick it up out of curiosity or are you looking for something particular in it, such as the solution of one of your own problems? Have you a plan of how you are going to read it? Are you going to take notes? Are you going to read for a set period of time, or are you just going to dip into it and go on reading until you have had enough?

The reason why I have started with these questions is because I would like you to be thinking very hard all the time you are reading this book. I believe that you will get the greatest possible benefit from it only if you have in mind a clear objective, and some kind of plan of how you are going to study what the book offers. If you have, why not take the simple but valuable further step of writing them down on a piece of paper so that you can be quite sure what they are? If you have no objective or plan at all, why not close the book for a few moments and try to decide what part of this subject you are interested in, and what will be the most useful or satisfying way to study it? Any objective and any plan will be better than none.

Another useful exercise to do at this juncture will be to think about your own views on what is meant by a problem and how problems can be solved. I suggest that you might

3

usefully give a little thought to that for comparison with the views expressed in this book.

The purpose of this chapter is to set the scene for the book as a whole by giving an explanation of the nature of problems, what they are and where they come from, and suggesting how we can have some control over the flow of problems that we have to contend with in life. The rest of the book will be concerned with a study of the various ways of being methodical in dealing with problems in general, and with problems of specific kinds.

THE CHARACTERISTICS OF PROBLEMS

What is a problem? What do we mean when we use the word problem? A problem is a kind of difficult situation. Let us consider a few typical examples of problematical situations and try to see what enables us to recognize that they are problems.

> My weight is a problem.
> Keeping my house in repair is a problem.
> I have a problem at work in recruiting staff.
> Fitting in all my regular meetings is a problem.

The reason why my weight is a problem is because I am fat and I would like to be thinner but I am unable to produce the desired effect. House repair is a problem because I want to get everything in good order but things go wrong faster than I can put them right. Recruiting staff is a problem because there is a shortage. Regular meetings are a problem because I want to attend all of them but there is not enough time.

There is no doubt that these situations are rightly called problems. What is significant about them as a class is that they have two features in common. In each there is, either stated or implied, an objective or a desired state of affairs and an obstacle which prevents me from getting things into the state in which I wish them to be.

I am not trying to set up a new definition of the word 'problem'. What it says in the dictionary is quite satisfactory as far as I am concerned. I am merely saying that all problems possess the two features I have just mentioned—an objective and an obstacle. If you have any difficulty in accepting that this is true, you might like to see whether you can find any examples of situations that appear to be properly regarded as problems, but which do not include an objective possessed by someone and an obstacle preventing the objective from being reached. As far as I have been able to ascertain, there are no problems that do not have both an objective and an obstacle somewhere in them.

THE ORIGINS OF PROBLEMS

A characteristic of primitive people is that they do not understand the origins of many of their problems. They are inclined to be superstitious and to attribute the origins of events and situations that they do not understand to supernatural powers. Conversely, a sign of civilization is that people understand much of what is happening to them, even though they may not have the power to overcome all their difficulties. However, even civilized people may be irrational, in so far as they may blame themselves or others or 'bad luck' for undesirable occurrences, when it might be more sensible to think carefully about how these originated for the sake of lessons that could be learnt for the future.

The origins of all human problems may be traced back to the various motives impelling us to action. These motives are of many kinds and of different degrees or levels of artificiality. The most basic and natural of them are the primary human drives such as the needs for self-preservation, food, and shelter. At a higher level of artificiality come such things as personal likes and dislikes, ambitions, and moral values, which we develop as we go through life. A third level consists of motives that we take over from other people, such as requests for help from our colleagues and instructions from our bosses. The connection with problems is that, unless we had these motives, we would never have any problems at all because we would never be trying to accomplish anything. To be without motives would be to be without life itself, because it would create a situation in which we lacked both the wish and the power to survive.

Unfortunately, or fortunately, according to one's point of

view, the world in which we live is arranged in such a way that our needs can seldom be satisfied directly or immediately from the resources available to us at any particular moment. We usually have to strive and to solve problems in order to get what we want. There also seems to be a natural law to the effect that if a person's wants become satisfied he very soon sets about developing new unsatisfied wants and in this manner maintains his own personal supply of problems.

THE EFFECT OF PROBLEMS ON THE QUALITY OF LIFE

It is sometimes painfully obvious that the quality of our lives is dependent upon the number and difficulty of the problems we have to face. Most of us try to find a balanced position somewhere between the tedium of a life in which there are no real problems to get our teeth into, and the stresses and strains of a life consisting of unceasing trouble, the latter being the side to which it is apparently easier to gravitate.

Anybody who can train himself to become an expert problem-solver is clearly in a position of advantage. He can tolerate a higher rate of intake of difficult problems because he can deal with them efficiently and take a detached view of them; and he can also do more about controlling the rate at which problems arise in his life because he understands their causation and can take precautions against them. What is more, the expert problem-solver may be able to find satisfaction in struggling with difficult problems like the chess masters who deliberately allow themselves to get into difficulties for the thrill of trying to get themselves out again, or the climbers who seek out more and more difficult ways of getting to the tops of mountains.

However, even if we cannot go so far as to become experts at solving problems, we should not overlook the fact that we have some freedom of choice regarding the extent to which we need to go on putting up with adverse circumstances. There is usually some possibility of getting out of an oppressive situation, and this is always worth considering when the going becomes rough. After all, it is not unheard of for prisoners to escape from confinement, or in the last resort for worms to turn. Alternatively, if we should find that we are making things difficult for ourselves by setting too high a standard in many of our endeavours and creating more problems than we can comfortably manage, the faster we realize this and take appropriate measures the sooner we shall be able to reduce our mental and physical workload to a tolerable level.

THE LIFE-CYCLE OF A PROBLEM

Although some problems seem to come upon us suddenly and just as suddenly disappear, it is characteristic of most problems that their comings and goings take place over a period of time. This fact can be traced back to the nature of our objectives and the obstacles that prevent us from reaching them.

Long before an objective becomes clear in our minds it may nevertheless have some sort of existence in a latent state. It may be little more than a vague intention or desire. Later it begins to develop, and then it increases in potency until it becomes active and impels us to do something. Then after a time it ceases to be fully active and begins to decline and we lose interest in it. Eventually the objective returns to a state of quiescence in which it is no longer a real influence on our behaviour. This pattern of growth and decay can also be seen in the life-cycle of an obstacle, but in this case we should perhaps speak of its 'effective state' rather than its 'active state' when referring to it at the height of its potency.

Suppose, for example, that a manager was not able to get some work done because his work-force had become depleted by the departure of a number of workers. It is unlikely that the objective, the doing of the work, came into existence overnight. It was probably foreseen and planned for over a considerable period, and whatever happened, it would only have faded slowly out of importance to become a thing of the past. It started off as something too far in the future to be thought about as a distinct piece of work to be accomplished. At this time it was in its latent state. When plans for getting the work done were being made it was in the developing state. When it was due to be done it was an active objective. When the end of the job was in sight it was in the declining state and when at last it was apparently all over and done with it had reached the quiescent state.

It was the same with the obstacle—the shortage of staff. The staff who departed must have taken some time to make up their minds to leave, and they probably resigned in ones and twos rather than all at once. When the staff were originally all at their posts, the obstacle was still latent and although some of them might have been on the way to becoming dissatisfied, or for other reasons beginning to think about giving up their jobs, there would have been no obvious sign by which the manager could have detected what was going on. Next, the

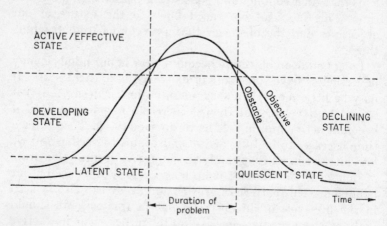

FIGURE 1. The life-cycle of a problem

obstacle developed, as the staff became slightly restive and one or two might have given notice to leave. In this state the obstacle might have been detectable in people's conversation and behaviour, although not yet affecting the firm's output. After the crucial loss of staff, however, the obstacle would have been effective. It would not then have been possible to cope satisfactorily with a workload of the size required. After a while, new recruitment of staff would have caused the obstacle to decline. And eventually when a sufficient number of staff had been replaced, the obstacle would have reverted to a state of quiescence where the work-force would have been restored and able to deal again with the normal run of tasks.

Figure 1 (p. 8) shows the life-cycle of a typical objective and obstacle in the form of a diagram.

Objectives and obstacles can come into conflict in a great variety of ways according to when they occur and how long they take to pass through the stages of growth and decay. It is easy to see that the worst situation occurs when the peak of effectiveness of the obstacle coincides with the peak of activity of the objective. This generates a problem which is both

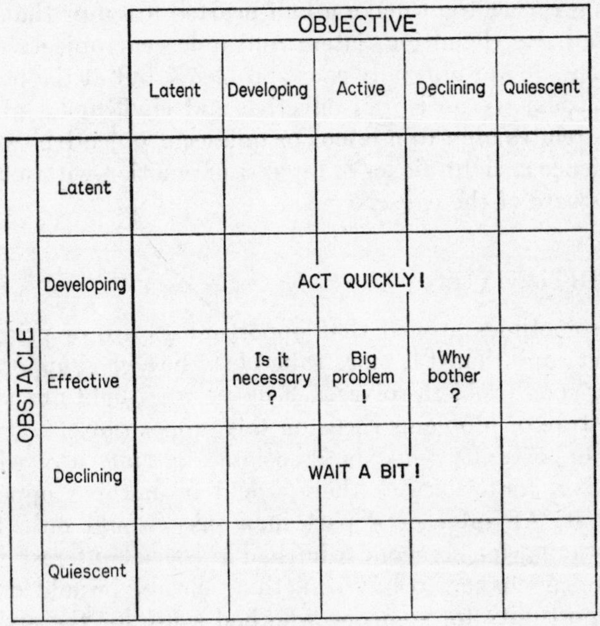

		OBJECTIVE			
		Latent	Developing	Active	Declining	Quiescent
OBSTACLE	Latent					
	Developing		ACT QUICKLY !			
	Effective		Is it necessary ?	Big problem !	Why bother ?	
	Declining		WAIT A BIT !			
	Quiescent					

FIGURE 2. Timing in problem-solving

important and difficult. It is not quite so easy to see what kinds of situation arise when obstacles and objectives come together in other ways, although it is instructive to consider the various possibilities. As there are five states in which either can be, there are in all twenty-five possible combinations. It would be tedious to describe them all separately, but by concentrating on the more interesting ones it is possible to simplify the picture to what is shown in Figure 2.

The point is that problems are certain to arise when active

objectives coincide with effective obstacles. While obstacles are developing the sooner they are attacked the better because they are getting more effective as time goes by, as when a boat is being launched on an ebbing tide. When obstacles are on the decline, however, it may be an advantage to wait until the task becomes easier, as when a grounded boat is floated away on a rising tide. When the objective is in either the developing or the declining state, the best policy may be to 'have a go' if it looks fairly easy, but otherwise it may be better to do nothing rather than make a half-hearted attempt that could well fail. By definition, latent and quiescent objectives and obstacles do not normally cause problems, but at the personal level, when we notice an effective and challenging obstacle which relates only to a latent or quiescent objective, we may experience a slight flicker of interest or emotion without being fully aware of the cause.

OPPORTUNITIES

It is sometimes argued that opportunities are of prime importance and that it is more valuable to be a good opportunist than a good problem-solver. Let us see what light our view of the nature of problems sheds on this proposition.

An opportunity must be associated in some way with an objective, for otherwise there would be nothing opportune about it. An offer of a part in a play would only be an opportunity for someone who had a special interest in the theatre. A chance to buy something cheaply would only be an opportunity for someone who had a use for the article in question.

There is often some kind of obstacle associated with an opportunity, because the person concerned may find it difficult to identify the objective or to see how to exploit or make the most of the opportunity. For example, a talented and presentable person may offer himself for employment. The employer may well face the obstacle that there is no suitable vacant post in which the applicant can be placed. This way of looking at an opportunity suggests that it is merely a new chance to make progress towards an existing objective and help to solve an existing problem, and it may have its own problematical aspects and need to be tackled just like any other kind of problem.

Skill at exploiting opportunities may be regarded as dependent upon the more general skill of problem-solving. To use it to the full we need a clear view of our long-term objectives and an awareness of ways by which they may be reached. If we know how to recognize what we are looking for, a quick look around from time to time will be enough to provide sufficient awareness to pick up most of the opportunities that come our way.

SUMMARY

In this chapter we have looked to see where problems come from and observed that they occur as a stream of situations generated by the interaction of our motives and our circumstances. Motives give rise to the objectives that we try to achieve, but circumstances may raise obstacles which bar our progress. The timing of the rise and fall in importance of objectives and obstacles affects the urgency with which we need to act. Our ability to exploit opportunities depends upon our skill at solving problems. Before going on to Chapter 2 here are some exercises for study which have been designed to give practice in the use of these concepts.

EXERCISES

1. If you knew, when reading p. 3, what your objective in reading this book was, what was it? In any case, what is your objective now?
2. Find two or more real problems that you or your friends face at present and write down the objective and obstacle in each instance.
3. In what ways could opportunities arise to enable the problems you have identified to be solved?
4. How could such problems be prevented from occurring in the future?
5. Describe the life-cycles of these problems.

2

The Methodical Approach
~

METHOD, PLANNING, AND THOUGHT

The purpose of this chapter is to introduce the principles of a methodical approach to problem-solving and to give a brief general description of how this approach can be used. Further details will be given in the later chapters.

To be methodical is to follow a definite method. It involves considering not only what one has to do but how to do it, and it involves a certain degree of control over one's actions.

A method is a set of actions designed or selected to help to solve a problem. It can be tailor-made to fit an unusual problem, or it can be a well-established pattern of action to be brought out when any situation arises to which it is applicable. The following are two of the more important of the many benefits of being methodical:

1. It increases the efficiency of our actions by preventing delays, avoiding waste of effort, and reducing the risk of making mistakes.
2. It helps to improve the quality of our work by making it easier to evaluate the effects of our actions.

The foundation of the methodical approach is the principle that careful planning improves the chances that action will be successful. This is widely believed in theory but unfortunately all too widely ignored in practice. We readily embark on all kinds of activities without questioning whether what we are doing is right or whether the way we are doing it is efficient.

To plan is to decide what to do before doing it. Like methods, plans can be specially made to fit circumstances or they can be ready-made for regular use in recurrent and familiar situations.

Deciding what to do requires thought. The nature of thought is a difficult subject and it is not appropriate to discuss it in depth in a book like this which sets out to be as practical as

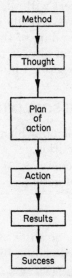

FIGURE 3. The effects of method on planning

possible. It is perhaps enough at this stage to observe that there are two different kinds of thought; that which goes on in consciousness and that which goes on in the unconscious workings of the brain. However, both may fairly be regarded as kinds of behaviour, and therefore it is not surprising that method can be as beneficial to mental behaviour as to physical behaviour.

Figure 3 shows the relationship between these various aspects of the situation. Method helps thought and leads to the production of a plan of action. Action leads to results, which we hope will to some extent be successful.

WORKING IN STAGES

The methodical approach is brought to bear by dividing the work of problem-solving into stages and concentrating upon one stage at a time. This makes it easier to work efficiently and to apply further and more specific methods at the right time.

The number of stages into which the solving of a problem is divided is not a matter of great importance. Many writers have suggested lists of stages with slight differences in number, meaning, and emphasis. What really matters is that we should have a thorough understanding of the sequence of operations so that we can learn it and always use it efficiently. The list below shows the stages described in this book.

STAGES OF PROBLEM-SOLVING

1. Formulating the problem, which involves its detection, identification, and definition.
2. Interpreting the problem.
3. Constructing courses of action.
4. Decision-making.
5. Implementation.

It is important to distinguish between these stages and to appreciate the value of proceeding by one stage at a time, as far as possible completing each one before starting the next. Although the whole sequence is a chain in which there should be no weak link, it is not always possible to follow it along in one go from beginning to end because problems themselves are not simple. Very often other problems appear on the way which need to be solved before further progress can be made, and sometimes more general problems are met which may make it necessary to revise our earlier assumptions and to return and repeat some stages that have already been worked through. Solving a problem is like going on a journey. It starts when we first realize that we have a problem to solve and it ends when the objective has been reached. An efficient method of problem-solving will ensure that every step of the work makes some kind of progress towards a solution.

STAGE 1. FORMULATING THE PROBLEM

The first stage is really three steps rolled into one. Before beginning to do anything about looking for a solution to the problem, we have to detect that it exists, identify the problematical aspects of the situation and then define the problem accurately. For instance, if the work of a group of people is impeded by the disruptive behaviour of a member of the group, the problem may not be attended to properly until someone has realized firstly that all is not well, secondly that a certain person is at the centre of it, and thirdly that the work of the group is being impeded by the behaviour of the person.

In most problems these steps are distinct and may be considered separately, but in some it may be necessary to take all three together. Sometimes the existence and identity of a difficult problem is all too obvious, and all that we need is to make an accurate definition in order to be able to make a good start. Consider the type of situation where something goes noticeably wrong. We may be sitting down at home reading a book and all the lights go out. Instantly we are aware of the existence of the problem and we can identify what kind of problem it is: a failure in the flow of electric current. But the way we define the problem will have a considerable influence on our actions to solve it. One definition, 'too many electric appliances switched on', for example, might cause us to go and inspect the fuses; another, 'meter empty', to find coins to insert in a meter; another, 'must finish this chapter', to light a candle; another, 'can't see any more', to change our activity from reading to conversation.

Sometimes a problem is presented to us formally by another person, who describes it in fairly definite terms and then we are left to get on with it. Someone may give us an unusual and difficult task to do, for instance. But it is more usual that our first impression of a problem is somewhat hazy and confused. It may be perceived merely as an uncomfortable feeling. In such a case we need to transform the sketchy and inadequate impression which indicates that we have some sort of a problem into a more objective statement that we can do something about. As an example of this, consider a child at school who is unable to understand what the teacher writes on the blackboard. The teacher complains of the child's 'slowness' and the child's parents gradually begin to realize that the child is not making progress and is unhappy at school. It may take some time for the parents to become aware that there is a problem here, and its true identity (perhaps that the child is short-sighted and cannot see what is on the blackboard) will have to be discovered before any kind of a useful start can be made towards putting matters right.

Defining the problem is the most important step of all in solving a problem. If we start work on the problem without being absolutely clear what it is, we are bound to waste time and effort on enquiries and activities which are not necessary and which will delay the mounting of an efficient attack on the true problem. I was present at a meeting of a club committee when an official asked for permission to buy some essential equipment. The response of the treasurer was to ask for a detailed list of equipment and prices to be submitted to the next meeting. This would have caused a delay of two months and a loss of opportunity to use the equipment during that period. It had to be pointed out to the treasurer, who was in effect creating a problem rather than solving one, that it would be possible to give the permission of the committee in general terms. It was finally agreed that the officials responsible for buying that particular kind of equipment should be empowered as a group to buy equipment of their choice up to the limit of a budget of £200. The real point at issue was how much the club could afford to spend on equipment, and the exact details of what was to be bought were not relevant to the making of this decision.

A further point is that anyone who knows exactly what his problem is is already half-way towards the solution. For example, a man ordered a roller-blind to fit a window. When it arrived it was too long. He could have sent it back and waited for another one, with loss of time and money, or sawn a piece off with risk of damaging it. But on reflection he realized it was really a problem of matching the length of the roller to the width of the window space, and that to widen the space would also be possible by drilling a hole to receive the spigot at the end of the roller. The solution had become obvious and was then accomplished by the use of available tools and skills.

The fact that in any problem there is an objective that is sought and an obstacle that prevents someone from reaching the objective, provides us with an effective formula for stating the definition of all problems. Simply to state what the objective and the obstacle are is sufficient definition for any problem.

Suppose, for example, that I am driving my car on my way to work, and when I come round a bend in the road I notice that a large tree has fallen across the road and blocked the way. I have a problem. My objective is to get to work at the usual time, but there is an obstacle, a tree that has blocked the road.

The objective is that which we really need to achieve. It is not always quite the same as what we are currently trying to achieve or what we have been hoping to achieve, because our intentions are occasionally misguided or biased. The obstacle is anything which is at present preventing us from reaching the objective. It may be something that can be seen and felt like a locked door or a punctured tyre, or it may be abstract like a lack of information or skill, or an incompatibility of one thing or person with another.

STAGE 2. INTERPRETING THE PROBLEM

The chances of finding a satisfactory solution to a problem are highest when the person trying to solve it understands it thoroughly. The second stage therefore is devoted to developing an understanding of the problem.

Let us consider for a moment what understanding means. For a problem-solver to have an understanding of the problem it is first necessary for the essential facts to be put into his mind. Next they must be brought into proper relationship with each other through a process which takes place mostly below the level of consciousness, but can be accompanied and strengthened by conscious reasoning. Only then will it be possible for his mind to make effective use of the information and produce a good solution.

Suppose, for example, that we have been shopping and are

faced with the problem of deciding whether or not we have been given the correct change. The essential facts are the price of the goods we bought, the amount of money we handed over, and the amount of change we were given back. The proper relationships between them are that the amount of change we were given back should equal the difference between the price of the goods and the amount of money we handed over. Unless we know the essential facts and can find the proper relationships between them we cannot be sure whether we have or have not been given the correct change. If we are inattentive, hard of hearing or unaccustomed to the monetary system, we may be missing some of the facts. If we are very young or uneducated or mentally handicapped we may not be clear about the proper relationships between the facts.

The same principle applies in problems of all degrees of difficulty and complexity. In an unfamiliar problem a good deal of careful analytical thinking may be required to identify the essential facts and analyse the relations between them. In many problems thought alone is insufficient and an investigation is needed to collect the information on which a sound understanding can be based.

It follows, therefore, that in order to reach a sound understanding more effectively, methods are needed to help discover and identify the essential facts and to bring out the significant relationships between them. Analysis is one such method we shall be considering.

We call this stage 'interpretation' because the problem-solver has to go through a process of explaining or interpreting the available information about the problem-situation to himself or others before he can complete his understanding.

STAGE 3. CONSTRUCTING COURSES OF ACTION

This stage includes the process of collecting ideas from various sources or generating new ideas of one's own and building all together into one or more possible courses of action. It should begin near where the second stage ends, at a point where an appreciable understanding of the problem situation has been attained.

In many instances the construction of courses of action is helped by the use of a replica or model of the situation in a manipulable or visible form. This can serve many useful purposes such as to test whether the problem is sufficiently well understood, to communicate understanding to other people, to stimulate ideas, to test theories, or to compare the merits of alternative courses of action.

STAGE 4. DECISION-MAKING

In real life few problems are found to have only one possible solution. The usual state of affairs is that several quite different promising courses of action can be identified and it then becomes necessary to make a choice between them. The decision-making stage is the stage which enables this choice to be made. Decision-making entails evaluating the proposed courses of action against the relevant criteria. The process often has to take account of uncertainty about the outcome of events that have not yet occurred, and it relies upon the ability to make sound judgements of the relative merits of the various possible outcomes. The decision-making stage is complete when the preferred course of action has been chosen and a firm commitment has been made to carry it out. Even when we have only one course of action to consider it is still necessary to make up our minds that we are going to act.

STAGE 5. IMPLEMENTATION

The final stage of problem-solving is the implementation of the chosen course of action. All the work done in the earlier stages may be wasted unless the chosen course is carried out properly. The implementation stage includes all the ways and means of ensuring that this is done.

The basis of implementation is detailed and thorough planning, by which one can ensure that the necessary resources are obtained and that a programme of action is drawn up. It must be arranged that all concerned have the information and skill required to do the job properly and are properly led and managed. The plan should include means of keeping control over the action to be taken so that any difficulties that may arise will be dealt with and action will continue until the objective has been reached. The plan must be flexible so that any further obstacles which may appear, or any changes which may take place in the objective, can be accommodated with a minimum of inconvenience.

To implement a course of action for solving a problem is to take the steps necessary to get from the current state of affairs in which the problem exists to another state where the objective has been reached. If other people are involved this may be a change of some seriousness for them. Success in implementation may therefore depend upon the care taken to help people to accept and adjust themselves to changes that are to take place.

Finally, when all is prepared, the plan has to be put into effect. Various kinds of control are necessary to ensure that what was decided is actually done. New difficulties are likely to be met because of obstacles encountered along the way, and these will give rise to distinct problems, each needing to be tackled methodically like any other. Eventually, one hopes, the objective or something closely equivalent to it will be reached.

Some of the methods available for solving problems are well known but not often used, and others are neither well known nor often used. This book sets out to help in remedying this state of affairs. Where ready-made methods are not available it is not usually difficult to invent them, and it is important to appreciate that even a crude method applied carefully can be more effective than an entirely haphazard approach.

SUMMARY

In this chapter we have looked at the relationships between method, planning, and thought, and the advantages of a methodical approach to problem-solving. We have introduced the idea of tackling the work of problem-solving by breaking it down into stages, and set the scene for the later chapters by explaining the purpose of

(1) Formulating the problem

(2) Interpreting the problem
(3) Constructing courses of action
(4) Decision-making
(5) Implementation.

EXERCISES

1. Consider a recent problem that you had to deal with. Write down a list of the stages through which you passed in trying to solve it. Compare this list with the five stages described in this chapter. Do they differ? If so, why?
2. Observe the behaviour and thought processes of other people when solving problems. Are they methodical?
3. Listen to a discussion, at work, at home, on the television or radio. Did the participants work methodically?
4. Consider a mistake someone has made, or any kind of failure. Could it have been avoided by a more methodical approach?
5. Take any problem and try to solve it methodically. Consider the difficulties encountered and try to understand their causes.
6. Invent a method for overcoming one of these difficulties.

3

Planning and Thinking on Paper

PLANNING AND PROBLEM-SOLVING

Planning is a powerful problem-solving technique which is valuable and effective in almost any situation. The only time when planning is not applicable is when the problem arises so suddenly and urgently that there is hardly time for any consideration at all. This occurs, for example, when we are crossing the road and a dangerous situation develops without warning and there is only enough time to leap away from the danger-spot as fast as possible. Apart from extreme instances of this type, it is always profitable to spend at least a little time in working out what is best to do in the circumstances, rather than to do the first thing that comes to mind. General Eisenhower was reputed to have said, 'In preparing for battle I have always found that plans are useless, but planning is indispensable'.

When a problem has been detected, the sooner we start planning how to deal with it the better. The plan will be tentative at first but it will develop and become more definite as more ideas and information become available. It will first be a foundation for preparing the attack and later on a guide to action. It is never too early to make a plan.

When the plan has been formed, the success of the chosen course of action will depend upon the care and skill put into the part of the plan dealing with implementation. In other words, the plan will have to cover everything of importance for making the chosen solution work.

If the problem being studied is not imminent, but is one expected to occur in the future, then most of the problem-solving task can be carried out as a planning activity. In this sense to plan is to solve a problem in advance so as to gain time for making preparations, so that preventive action may be taken before the situation can become serious, or so that it can be prevented from becoming a real problem at all.

DO WE SPEND ENOUGH TIME IN PLANNING?

The plain fact is that most of us do not do as much planning as we ought to. We leave too many actions unplanned and when we do plan we do not start soon enough and we are not thorough enough and we do not look far enough ahead.

Examples of events that we commonly under-plan are meetings, investigations, and communications. It is interesting to note that these are all activities where the reactions of other people are important.

For each one of us, according to the nature of his work and circumstances, there is a proportion of time that should be devoted to planning, including planning the use of time itself. The way to find out the correct amount is by trying out different policies and carefully evaluating the results. In many cases it will be found that we get better results by tackling fewer problems and doing more planning.

There are some people who object that too much planning can be a bad thing and that it is wrong to encourage people to do more of it. They say, for example, that when they go on holidays they do not like their activities to be planned out in detail; they would rather take things as they come and be free and easy. They do not like to be regimented. Some people do not like parties and similar social gatherings to be in any way organized; they prefer such events to be casual and un-premeditated and to develop naturally. But let us be quite clear about what is in question here. Planning or any other way of being methodical is not at all compulsory; it is just an aid which is available for use when we need it. In circumstances where we do not want its effects it would be absurd to apply it.

The satisfaction of emotional needs related to the desire for freedom as expressed, for example, in adventure, surprise, and wonder, is probably essential for human well-being. When we have a need for this kind of satisfaction and we see that planning would be disadvantageous then, clearly, it should be avoided. However, it is quite often true that even the search for freedom or originality can be helped by planning of the right kind. For example, is it reasonable to argue that the planning of a mountain-climbing expedition or a voyage of exploration detracts from the quality of the adventure experienced by those who take part? What beautiful picture, what magnificent building, was not planned? It is the purpose of the planning that matters; it must be based on a clear and true understanding of our objective.

HOW TO MAKE A PLAN

Although the form of a plan will differ according to its purpose and circumstances, we may consider a few important features which should be covered or at least thought about in the preparation of most kinds of plan.

1. State the main objective. In a plan to be passed to other people as part of their instructions it may also be desirable to give a general review of the problem-situation.
2. State in general terms how the objective will be achieved, explaining what principles are to be followed and what constraints apply to the solution.
3. Break down the main objective into parts and say in greater detail how they will be achieved.
4. Estimate the resources of money, materials, people, and time that will be required. Plan how these are to be obtained.
5. Prepare a programme showing the sequence and timing of the actions required. Build flexibility into it.
6. Formulate the plan in action terms, stating who does what.
7. Check the plan for completeness and accuracy.
8. Rehearse actions which are likely to be difficult or whose outcomes are difficult to predict.

Many suggestions in the chapters which follow will show how the above steps can be accomplished, especially in Chapter 14 on preparing for implementation, where the planning required to put the solution of a problem into action will be described in some detail. Objectives will be discussed in Chapter 4 and how to achieve them in Chapters 8, 9, and 10. Contingencies are sure to arise as the plan develops, and any of the whole range of problem-solving techniques and methods may be needed to deal with them.

THINKING ON PAPER

Successful planning depends on the ability to think ahead and think clearly. Thinking is basically an easy process, but it is inclined to become confusing when we try to handle a large number of ideas all at once. Writing is another basically easy process and can be used as an aid to clear thinking. By transferring thoughts onto paper, writing enables us to pre-serve them for future use instead of leaving them to be obliterated by the onward rush of new thoughts arriving in consciousness. If we write our ideas down we can hold onto them, we can sort them out at leisure and we can pick out some for further attention and so concentrate on what we believe to be important. This process of helping the mind to handle information may conveniently be called 'thinking on paper', a term which I believe was coined by my old friend and colleague J. U. M. Smith.

Although ideas worth recording may occur to us at any time, such as when waiting for a bus, or in the middle of a meeting, difficult mental work can only be done to order in relatively good conditions. Just what the appropriate condi-tions are is a matter which differs from person to person and, as in so many similar situations, what we should do is to find out what suits us best and then make sure that we get it when the need arises. In Chapters 5 and 8 we shall discuss at greater length the effect of surroundings and other conditions on thinking.

The proverbial medium for jotting down ideas is the back of an old envelope, but this has practical limitations. It is always useful to carry a pocket notebook ready for use, and when we are in the office or at home a board with some sheets of writing paper clipped to it is a valuable piece of equipment. For some kinds of work it is handy to have a board large enough to take two pieces of paper side by side.

With pen and paper at the ready, then, we set out to put our thoughts on paper. The first thing to do is to set down the objective. The form of the statement of objective is not really important. It will vary according to circumstances, and could be like any of the following, for instance.

A new form of organization for the finance department.
How to fit out a storage cupboard.
A new fund-raising scheme.
How to get rid of an old boat.
'Careers in estate management'—a talk to school leavers.
Where to go for a fishing/camping holiday.
My next five years.

If something approaching a statement of objective comes to mind, we write it down immediately, regardless of how crude or unsatisfactory it may seem. Any attempt, once set down, can easily be improved whereas it is very difficult to carry an idea in consciousness and try to improve it at the same time. Later on, the objective can be polished up when better ways of expressing it are thought of. It is not necessary to find obstacles immediately because there may not be any. However, if we are clearly aware of the nature of an obstacle at the outset, this may as well be written down without delay.

The next thing to do is to write down some ideas associated with the objective we have identified. We should not try to judge whether these ideas are useful or not. The immediate purpose is to express them and put them where they can be scrutinized methodically. Not all of the thoughts we express in this way will be entirely relevant to the objective, but that does not matter. If they were not allowed to come out they might possibly interfere with the flow of new ideas. In any case, they may come in useful later on in some other context.

After a number of ideas have been recorded it usually begins to become apparent that several of them are similar in some respects. They are linked by a common characteristic or seem to belong to a certain class. We can try, then, to find a word or two to denote the name of the class, and write this down as a heading. Then we can see whether there are any more examples of the same class already written down, or which can be thought up deliberately, and add them to the list. Here is an example of the sort of results that this process typically produces, to show the underlying train of thought and how an understanding of the situation can develop.

EXAMPLE OF THINKING ON PAPER

Objective: *To make grass grow in the bare patches on my lawn.*
What makes me think of it?—Seeing the variegated state of the village football pitch.

Ideas

Buy some more grass seed.
The birds ate most of the last lot.
The weather was too dry the last time I tried to make it grow on the bare patches.
The lawn needs aerating.
It should be done in a rainy period.
There was a bird-deterrent on the last lot but it might have got washed off when we watered it.
The village football pitch is very bare of grass except around the white marking lines, where it is remarkably lush and green.

Aspects

Soil conditioning.	Spike the ground.
	Rake it.
	Add peat and sand.
	Lime it, to produce the effect seen on the football pitch.
Watering.	Wait until a rainy day.
Bird damage.	Sow plenty for the birds.
Other damage.	Don't mow it for a while.
	Use the lawn as little as possible. Keep off the grass!
	Remove weeds from bare patches.

In many cases it is possible to see a pattern emerging in the list of headings. Some of them may be seen to be related to each other. When this happens, we can make further progress by finding out exactly what the relationships are and adjusting the classes to form a meaningful pattern or sequence. At this stage we may become aware that one or more of the classes do not fit well, or that there are some gaps in the system that could be closed by bringing in further classes to complete the picture.

RECOGNIZING COMMON TYPES OF PROBLEM

By the time a clear pattern of headings with orderly lists of ideas under them has been produced we may feel that we are beginning to understand the subject. We can then try to recall from our past experience any useful principles that we may know to be applicable to this particular subject. We may recognize not only the subject but also the type of problem we are up against, and then be able to recall principles applying to that. Here are some examples of common types of problem.

CONTROL PROBLEMS

A very common type of problem is the problem of control. This occurs when we are trying to get somebody or something to behave in a particular way or to a certain standard of performance, and he or it does not always do what we want. We should remember that the first essential in a situation like this is to be clear about the standard of performance required, and to ensure that what is expected has been explained to any person concerned. To give an example, I was once asked for advice about the training of staff in 'customer service', which means behaving towards customers in the attentive, pleasant, and helpful way that customers desire and expect. One aspect of this which we then talked about was whether or not the staff who dealt with customers greeted them with a smile. It was admitted that this was not happening as much as it should. 'Well then', I said, 'If this is what you want, you must explain to staff that it is required of them. Do you

tell them that they are expected to smile at the customers?'
'No, we do not', was the answer, 'Surely any well-brought-up
person knows that it is correct to greet customers with a
smile!'

But the fact is that people cannot be expected to behave
in a particular way merely because we think that they ought
to. They need to be informed of what we wish them to do and
even this is no guarantee that they will be able to comply.
There may be many difficulties facing them of which we are
quite unaware, and they may have motives of their own
which lead them in other directions.

If it is a thing that is to be controlled it is essential that it
is properly set up to do what is needed, and thereafter it is
more a matter of routine to monitor performance and take
corrective action as required.

Good control is more easy to achieve when there is inherent
stability in the system. It is possible to ride a bicycle with
'no hands' because of the stability produced by the castering
action of the front wheel. If a group of people can find common objectives this will exert a similar stabilizing influence
and help them to move forward together without the need for
external control.

PERSONAL DIFFERENCES

As another example, we may identify a problem as a situation
where we have a decision to make but there are several
people involved, and it is not clear which one we should most
try to satisfy. We may then recognize that this is a typical
kind of problem caused by a difference between personal
objectives. We may have learned from experience that in
such a problem it is helpful to identify the people concerned
and write down lists of their respective objectives. It then
becomes relatively easy to decide whose objectives are the
ones to go for.

SEARCHING

Yet another example is where we recognize that we are
thinking about a situation where a search is required. Searches

may take many forms such as a literature search, a search for a lost object, a person to fill a vacancy, a new product, a new technique, and so on. However, the principles of efficient searching are much the same regardless of the nature of the thing being sought.

Here is a list of principles of searching, the headings of which have been taken from *An Introduction to Scientific Research*, by E. Bright Wilson. Although these come from a book mainly about laboratory research they can be applied to all kinds of search.

1. Know as much as possible about the object of search.
   This will help us to distinguish it from its surroundings and to devise appropriate procedures for locating it. If someone has lost a pet animal, for instance, the more we know about its habits and appearance the easier it will be to anticipate where it might have gone and to see it when it comes into our field of view.

2. Prove, if possible, that the object exists in the area to be searched.
   If rescuers at a mining accident know that the people they are trying to find are still alive and are confined to a certain area, their efforts are likely to be more concentrated and determined than otherwise.

3. Use the most efficient method of detection.
   Provided that it is economic to do so, a method of searching should be adopted which is sensitive to the characteristics of the object. For example, if we are searching for a criminal with a scar on his hand it would be appropriate to look at the hands of all suspects. If we are looking for a needle on the carpet we may find it more easily with a magnet than by eye.

4. Be sure you would see the object if it were encountered.
   This means that we should maintain our vigilance at all times while the search is on. It may be necessary to introduce spurious signals to make sure that the system of detection is still working.

5. Be sure you wouldn't see the object when it isn't there.
   An over-sensitive detection system will produce false alarms. A person who is always having 'brilliant new

ideas' may be more nuisance than help, and a person with a 'chip on his shoulder' will see inadequacy in other people when others would not.

6. Search systematically instead of haphazardly.

We are often capricious in our searches, looking twice in some places and not at all in others. Instead, we ought to plan and follow a systematic route.

7. If possible, devise a way of determining the approximate direction and distance of the object at every point of search.

In the traditional game of 'hunt the thimble', the searcher is guided by cries of 'warmer' or 'colder' from the on-lookers. When we are weighing objects in a balance the way the needle swings tells us whether to add or subtract weight as we search for the correct combination of weights.

8. In many-dimensional problems it is usually necessary to devise a one-dimensional path.

If something has been lost in a large area it is useful to divide it up into small areas and search them one at a time, in a definite sequence. If we are trying to count sheep or salmon we cause them to pass through a narrow place in single file. When trying to open a combination lock, adjust a television receiver or a carburettor, it is better to alter only one of the controls at a time than to juggle with all together at once.

9. If possible, mark the starting point, and record the path actually followed.

Otherwise we may forget what we have done and lose valuable information which could have guided the later stages of the search.

10. Use a convergent procedure.

We should try to use a procedure which closes in on the object, so that the chances of finding it will increase as the search develops. When looking for a fault in a piece of equipment, we may be able to proceed by a series of tests which eliminate one area after another until the fault is reached, removing as large as possible a portion of the remainder at each step.

11. Search the most probable place first.

This is obvious enough, but when we are searching in the most probable place we are sometimes over-hasty and fail to notice that the object is there.

12. Distribute the available time, facilities, or effort in reasonable proportions in different regions.

When there is not enough time or effort to search any one place thoroughly, we might as well use it all for searching the most probable place. Otherwise we should share it out, trying to arrange that if a place is to be searched at all, enough resources are allocated to it so that we can find out with reasonable certainty whether the object is there or not.

13. Take into account the finite probability of missing the object on passing by it.

If we do not see something it does not follow that it is not there. It might be worthwhile to have a second look. Problems for which a solution could not be found yesterday might be soluble today because circumstances have changed.

14. Consider any effect the search procedure may have on the search object.

If the object is a living creature, it is very likely to react to being searched for and run away or change its behaviour, according to whether it wants to be found or not. If the object is inanimate it may also be changed for better or worse by the process of search. The search can cause a fault where there was none before or conceal one that is present.

PROBLEMS CAUSED BY AMBIGUITY

When struggling with our thoughts we realize sometimes that we have got two or more ideas mixed up together. This is very likely to be the cause of the trouble whenever we notice that we have feelings of confusion. What usually has happened is that we have been caught out by an ambiguous term or expression. One name is being applied to two different ideas or things. The principle to be applied here is very simple. If some ideas are confused, separate them! All that we need to do is to write down a description of one of the ideas on its own and then the other. It then becomes relatively easy to see the difference between them, and to decide whether the ambiguous term can truly be applied to either or should be avoided. Finally, to make sure that the ideas remain separate in our thinking in the future, it is wise to find more satisfactory names for them. As an example, I recall the experience of trying to sort out a confusion in my own thoughts about the idea of planning. I found that I was having trouble because the word 'planning' seemed sometimes to lead me to think about one kind of thing and sometimes another. As it was a matter that I needed to be able to understand clearly and be able to discuss clearly, I naturally wanted to get to the bottom of it. When, after a while, I realized that this was a case of two ideas with the same name, I saw that I ought to apply the principle of separation. By writing down one idea first and then the other I was able to identify the true kind of planning, where one decides what to do before doing it, and distinguish it from the extra idea masquerading under the name of planning, which was in fact 'thinking on paper'.

PRINCIPLES FOR SOLVING COMMON TYPES OF PROBLEM

Once the type of situation we are in has been recognized and we have remembered the principle to be applied, the all-important next stage is to make sure that we do apply the principle to the situation. This requires an effort of will and the determination to persevere with the task until the desired results are obtained. In the case of a search we have to go on searching until either we have found what we are looking for, or else have proved beyond doubt that it is not there at all. The only satisfactory reason to give up a search is to realize that the problem is not a search problem after all, such as when we suddenly remember that we have thrown away the thing that we are looking for!

But, one may fairly ask, where do such wise principles as those we have been discussing come from? The answer is that they come from the study of problems. In each instance they have been derived from experience by somebody who thought carefully about what he had seen and done and heard, and who extracted a permanent lesson from it which can be applied whenever the circumstances repeat themselves. Any intelligent person can do this. It is a matter of taking what I call a professional view of life. We can also collect useful principles by reading about the subjects with which we are concerned and by discussing our problems with others who have been through similar experiences.

Not everything that we may try to think out on paper will turn out to be a difficult problem. The process of writing it down may in fact be sufficiently effective in clarifying the issue to indicate what we ought to do. However, it is to be expected that some issues will remain stubborn and problematical. In such cases we can choose either to concentrate upon the difficulty and mount a full-scale attack on it, or to regard it as a side-issue and make a note of it for later attention, and push on with an exploration of other matters which are more important or more amenable.

If we choose to deal there and then with a problem that we have identified, we have available the methods of problem-solving described in this book. Most of them fit in very well and form a powerful combination with the technique of thinking on paper.

If we have a lot to write, it will help to use abbreviations for long words that we use frequently. It is also an advantage to use a system of notation to help in picking out the different kinds of ideas under consideration. One way of doing this is to label the more important ideas that have been written, with a sign or symbol, which indicates what we intend to do about them. Initial letters are useful for this purpose, such as 'A' which means that it is to be acted upon, 'P' for problem, 'O' for objective, and 'Q' for a question that needs an answer. To make the most of this method it helps to leave ample margins at each side of the paper in which to put the notation signs.

The final stages of thinking on paper are simply to tidy up the ideas that have been produced, by crossing out what is not worth retaining and putting the remainder into logical order to make it ready for the next step of further consideration or action.

SUMMARY

In this chapter we have seen that planning and problem-solving go hand-in-hand. Problem-solving is aided by planning and in planning we frequently have to solve problems in advance.

When, in the course of planning, we are able to record our thinking on paper, we are in a better position to benefit from our mental labours because written thoughts can be retained in view and reconsidered at leisure.

In our planning and thinking on paper we shall often recognize types of problem, such as control problems, problems of personal differences, searching, and problems caused by ambiguity, which can be tackled by applying general principles that we know to be useful.

EXERCISES

Before we move on to the chapters dealing in detail with the stages of problem-solving, here are a few more practical exercises to work on. Their purpose is to provide a little experience of a disciplined approach to planning, so that the practical value of each step can be appreciated.

1. Think about one or two events that have affected your life recently and consider whether they occurred by chance or as a result of good or bad planning. What can you conclude from this about the need to make plans carefully?
2. Prepare a brief plan for each of the following actions, following out as far as possible the eight steps listed earlier in this chapter.
   (*a*) How you will spend the next weekend.
   (*b*) How you will spend your next day at work.
   (*c*) How to obtain something that you need.
3. The next time you face a problem, try 'thinking on paper' as described in this chapter as a method of attack.

Stage 1

FORMULATING THE PROBLEM

4

Formulating the Problem

This is the first of a group of chapters dealing with the main stages of problem-solving. Formulating the problem may be difficult and may take a long time to do properly in some situations, but it is of great importance. Einstein once wrote that 'the formulation of a problem is often more essential than its solution, which may be merely a matter of mathematical or experimental skill'. He was thinking mainly about problems in physics at the time, but the proposition applies equally well to other fields. In business, for example, once a problem has been correctly formulated, the solution may often be found to consist of the application of one or other well-tried principles or techniques of management.

The purpose of this chapter is to discuss what can be done to get to grips with a problem and how to start clarifying the situation in which the problem is found. To meet these purposes we shall have to consider how to detect and to identify problems and how to make a precise definition of any problem that is going to be tackled.

DETECTING THE PROBLEM

No systematic or methodical work can be done towards the solution of a problem until its existence has been detected, just as no doctor can cure us of a disease until someone has noticed that we are ill.

We are familiar with the situation often seen in a Western drama, where the cowboy hero is waylaid by villains. He rides in a carefree manner along the valley trail, not knowing that the rustlers, Indians, bandits, etc., are preparing an ambush for him up in the rocks ahead. The drama of the situation derives from the fact that our hero is in a situation of rapidly increasing danger, but continues to be unaware of it and consequently takes no precautions to defend himself. However, once the sound of a few rifle shots and ricochets comes to his ears, the situation reverses, and he leaps into action and sets about his new task of turning impending doom into victory.

The lesson we can learn from situations like this is that we should try to be alert and vigilant for signs of trouble, so that we can take precautions at the earliest possible stage. By this means we may not only prevent the problem from growing in seriousness or difficulty, but we may also save time by being able to deal with the situation sooner than later. This is not to be construed as advice to be over-cautious or permanently apprehensive. It is only a reminder of the importance of being able to recognize the signs of real danger and to react to them quickly and firmly.

A far more significant example is the real-life problem of protecting beaches from pollution by oil from ships. Although we have suffered an increasing amount of beach pollution over the last few decades, and been aware of the increasing quantity of oil that is carried by sea, we did not take steps either to avert the danger or to develop methods of cleaning the beaches, until several disasters had already occurred.

There are two ways by which potential problems can be prevented from becoming serious. One is to make a study of problems in general and become an enthusiast at detecting and solving them. This will help us to take a healthy attitude towards problems. We shall be keen to tackle any situation that gives the appearance of presenting a problem and deal with it promptly rather than do nothing and hope that the problem will go away. In other words, it will enable us to take a more positive and aggressive attitude towards any sign of a problem that may appear. The other approach is to make a study of the signs and symptoms of the sorts of problems that are of the greatest importance to us individually, in other words, to strive to become experts in our own particular fields of work.

How to Detect Problems

To detect a problem is to become aware of its existence and to recognize that it is a problem. In order to be skilful at detecting problems we need to learn how to recognize a wide variety of problem-situations and to react in an appropriate manner to them.

We first need to consider what forms problem-situations can take, so that we know what we are looking for. Problem-situations can be divided into six basic types, as follows.

1. A feeling of dislike towards something or an urge to get away from it.
2. A feeling of desiring something or an urge to achieve it.
3. A feeling of dislike of one thing coupled with a desire for another, or an urge to change.
4. An impression that there is a barrier to getting away from something.
5. An impression that there is a barrier to some achievement.
6. An impression that there is a barrier to change.

We need to get into a habit of reacting to feelings and impressions of all these kinds by perceiving that we are in a problem-situation which needs to be properly identified and defined. Whenever we find ourselves in one of these six different situations we should say to ourselves, 'Here is a problem. What makes it problematical?'

Here is an example of a typical situation where it is valuable to be able to realize that a certain form of difficulty indicates a certain sort of problem. We may be writing a letter or a report and come to a stage where the flow of words begins to slow down. We feel frustrated, perhaps confused, or perhaps our attention wanders away from the task in hand. What is happening? What should we do?

What is happening is that a barrier to our progress has arisen. What we should do is to recognize this and seek out the cause of the trouble, otherwise we may lose concentration and continue to fall prey to every little distraction that comes along. The trouble may be that we are attempting to use the wrong form of expression for the idea we have in mind, or that we are saying something which contradicts something else we want to say. If we stop trying to write and start trying to find the obstacle to progress and to remove it, we may be able to clear the problem up quickly and make progress again, but if we just try to struggle on we may continue to be confused and to make little progress.

HOW TO IDENTIFY PROBLEMS

Having detected that we have a problem, the next step is to identify it in order to single it out for investigation. If it is a simple problem this is an easy matter, but if it is a complex one its identification may be a task of great difficulty.

However, it is easy enough to make a start in the right direction towards identifying the problem. All we have to do is to ask suitable questions, according to the type of situation in which we have detected the problem.

1. What is it that we dislike? What are we trying to get away from?
2. What is it that we desire? What are we trying to achieve?
3. What is it that we dislike and what do we desire instead? What changes do we wish to make?
4. What is preventing us from getting away from the situation that we dislike?
5. What is preventing us from achieving what we desire?
6. What is preventing us from changing from what we have now to what we want to have?

When we have found the answer to the appropriate one of these questions we shall know in which direction the solution lies.

DEFINING THE PROBLEM

But the first stage of problem-solving is not finished until we have defined the problem clearly and made quite sure that our definition is both correct and complete. In Chapter 2 we touched briefly on this subject, but there will be no harm in going over it again in more detail because it is the most important step of all in problem-solving.

Here are some of the advantages of having a clear definition of a problem.

1. It enables us to concentrate on what really matters.
2. It helps us to avoid wasting time on irrelevancies.
3. It gives us a better chance to evaluate the success of our achievements because it helps us to be clear about what we are trying to do.
4. It helps us to explain to other people what we are trying to do.
5. It helps us to avoid working at cross-purposes with other people.
6. It gives us confidence.
7. It gives us a clear aim.
8. It gives us a choice of strategies, for example either to avoid the obstacle or to remove it (this point will be dealt with more fully in Chapter 8).
9. It often gives a direct clue as to what kind of course of action will be successful in solving the problem. For example, if the objective is to reach a certain standard of performance then we may recognize that this is a problem of control, and there are certain well-established principles for solving problems of that kind, which were mentioned briefly in Chapter 3 under the heading of 'Control Problems' and will be discussed at greater length in Chapter 15 under various headings.

OBJECTIVE AND OBSTACLE

All problems have the two outstanding features of an objective that someone is trying to reach and an obstacle that is preventing him from reaching it. The key to the solution of any problem can be found in a clear definition of the problem in terms of the objective and the obstacle. In recent years I have been able to observe a considerable number of managers at work on the solution of problems during training courses. It has been obvious that those who really try to define their problems in this manner tend to make good progress towards their solution, whereas those who do not try or who cannot define them in this way tend not to get very far.

Here are a few examples to show how it can be done, with easy and difficult problems.

1. Suppose that a manager has a problem in selecting a suitable person to fill a vacancy. His objective is to find someone who will be able to do a certain job very well. His obstacle is that he does not know anybody who has the required abilities and at the same time is looking for a new job.
2. Suppose that a manufacturer wants to increase the size of his factory but has no ready funds for the purpose. The former is his objective and the latter is his obstacle.

In both of the above examples the problem is clearly understandable and the objective and the obstacle are obvious. The next examples are more difficult.

3. Suppose that our boss is talking to us and he says, 'Now that the new sub-station has been running for several months I think that you ought to go and have a look at it.' What are the objective and obstacle here? The objective is to produce what the boss wants, but what does he want? Presumably he wants a report, either spoken or written, but what should it contain? The obstacle, in the first place, is that we don't know exactly what he does want. We would be foolish to proceed without asking him for further details.
4. Pursuing the earlier example of difficulty in writing, suppose that we are writing a letter to ask for some kind of assistance. We complete the first couple of paragraphs and then the flow of words begins to slow down and eventually stops. What is happening? We originally wanted to obtain assistance—objective 1. We decided to ask a certain person for it—objective 2. We decided that we would need to write a letter—objective 3. But now an obstacle has appeared in the way. What is it? Is it that we do not know how to proceed, or rather that we have lost the thread of our argument? If the latter, why have we lost it? Perhaps it is because we don't know what idea to put forward next, or because we cannot find a suitable mode of expression, or

because we have become distracted by some side-issue, or because what we want to say clashes in some way with what we have already written. The sooner we identify the true obstacle the quicker we shall be able to deal with it and make progress again.

While we are on the subject, here is a useful tip for dealing with this kind of problem in writing. If we have been writing fluently and then find ourselves beginning to slow down or to become confused, we should not force ourselves to continue to produce nothing but our very best prose. It is better to stop thinking about the rightness or wrongness of what we are writing and take a new piece of paper on which to set down quickly all the thoughts that we currently have in mind, no matter what they may be. Being on a different piece of paper, this material will not obstruct what we have previously been writing. We should not look back over the new page until we have quite run out of ideas. If some of the ideas seem to be about quite different subjects they should still be written down, as in 'thinking on paper', because they might be of considerable value in a more appropriate context. Next we can read through what we have done, cross out what is wrong and make any further corrections that may appear to be necessary. We can then take what we need of this material and edit it back into the original piece of writing which gave rise to the difficulty.

Some people find this procedure a considerable aid to fluency and a help to getting more enjoyment from writing. It works because it frees the flow of ideas which have become stuck in a mental bottleneck. We cannot easily do several things at once, so when we are trying to collect our ideas on a particular topic, put them into the best possible sequence, and express them in perfect English at the same time, we are trying to do the impossible.

5. The same sort of thing often happens in the conduct of a meeting, when a dozen highly paid executives are prevented from being productive by the introduction of a 'red herring' in the discussion. The chairman of the meeting should deal quickly with this obstacle, which is a serious matter because it may cause a great deal of valuable time

to be wasted if it is allowed to hold up the proceedings. The objective might be to reach a decision on an important issue. The obstacle might be that Mr. So-and-so has started up a new discussion on a topic that is not relevant to the agreed business of the meeting.

In these last examples the problem is embedded in the situation fairly deeply, and needs to be brought out and expressed clearly in order to set up a satisfactory basis on which to build a solution.

In the example of the sub-station we must be clear about what kind of investigation the boss requires us to undertake; in writing a letter we can get out of a muddle by defining what we are trying to achieve and what is preventing us; in a meeting the man who wastes our time will understand if the chairman explains that certain topics are irrelevant to the main purpose. Incidentally, in situations like these, it is unlikely that the problem would have arisen in such a severe form if the overall objective had been defined clearly at the outset.

As one last example, here is a problem of a type which is particularly difficult to define.

6. An airline company had bought some new aircraft, and these were required by law to be weighed accurately at regular intervals. The aircraft were of the latest design and very large and heavy, so heavy in fact that to weigh them was beyond the capacity of all the company's weighing equipment. The process of weighing aircraft takes them out of service for several days, it is laborious, and it was believed by the company not to be at all essential for practical purposes, because the aircraft are always weighed by the manufacturer before sale and it is possible to calculate with reasonable accuracy subsequent changes in weight caused by modifications and other accumulations of material. The company did not in fact wish to weigh the new aircraft at all and would not have considered doing so if it had not been for the requirements of the law. What is the best way to define this problem? There seem to be a number of different ways, according to the way that we look at the situation.

 (i) The objective is to meet the requirements of the law. The obstacle is the wish not to weigh the aircraft.
 (ii) The objective is to avoid weighing the aircraft. The obstacle is that the law says it must be done.
(iii) The problem is that there are two conflicting objectives (and there is no obstacle as such).
(iv) There are two objectives: to meet the requirements of the law and to avoid weighing the aircraft. The obstacle is that these are incompatible.

Of these alternatives the first two are clearly the weakest, because they depend upon assumptions about priorities which we have insufficient information to justify; we do not know which ought to be regarded as the objective and which the obstacle. The third would be an exception to the general principle that all problems have both an objective and an obstacle, and the fourth seems to be the most satisfactory and to present the essentials of the problem in the clearest possible manner.

GETTING THE DEFINITION RIGHT

Since it may take some time to get the definition of the problem right it is advisable to start with a preliminary definition and restate it more accurately when our understanding of the problem has progressed.

One way to probe into the problem-situation to improve on the accuracy of a definition or prevent an incomplete definition from being accepted uncritically is to ask questions such as the following.

1. Is this the only objective, or are there others which this obstacle prevents us from reaching?
2. Is this objective desired for its own sake, or is it just a way to reach a further objective?
3. Do we really need to reach this objective?
4. What will happen if we reach this objective?
5. If we reach this objective, will the problem then be solved?
6. Does this obstacle really prevent us from reaching the objective?
7. If we overcome this obstacle will it then be possible to reach the objective?

Here are some examples from real life which have been shown by this questioning technique to require re-definition.

1. A manager had the objective of improving his productivity by five per cent (compound) every year. At first he listed the following as obstacles:
   (a) labour shortage
   (b) absenteeism
   (c) lack of incentives for the labour force
   (d) restricted output capacity of the plant
   (e) restriction on capital expenditure on new plant.
   After questioning he found that (a) was not an obstacle but an incentive to solve the problem. He also found that (d) was not always the limiting factor and that (e) was not entirely true.

2. In a manager's initial definition of a problem he said that his objective was to reduce the number of working hours in his factory from 40 to 35 per week because of a trade union agreement, maintaining the same standards of production as before. He thought that the obstacle was the consequent rise in costs. After questioning he revised his definition, realizing that the objective was really to maintain the existing level of output and costs and the obstacle was the enforced reduction in working hours.

3. In this example the real objective was hidden underneath layers of intervening objectives, each one of which had to be penetrated by questioning until the ultimate one was reached. A consultant was requested to explain to an enquirer how to perform certain mathematical calculations. 'What for?' asked the consultant. 'Because I need the results in the design of an electronic circuit.' 'What is the purpose of the electronic circuit?' 'It is for use in a controlling device.' 'What is to be controlled?' 'A machine tool for making . . . . . .' The final question was, 'Why don't you just buy the machine tool you need from the . . . . Tool Company, where they are available from stock?'

$P = O + O$

Here is a simple mnemonic to help remember to define a

problem in terms of objective and obstacle: $P = O + O$. P is the problem, one O is the objective and the other is the obstacle. This is the universal formula which expresses symbolically the common properties of problems in the most concise possible form.

In the process of definition we are constructing something like an equation, in which one side is the difficult situation that we conceive to be the problem and the other side is the definition that we are formulating in terms of objective and obstacle. At first the two sides may be out of balance because our definition does not fit our concept of the problem. When we have altered the definition so that it fits, we may then realize that what we have been thinking about is not the true problem, or is not the whole problem, or is somebody else's rather than our own. This will give rise to a new concept that will throw the equation out of balance again and indicate that we need to revise the definition to make it fit our new view of the problem. By successive approximations we improve both sides alternately and make progress towards an acceptable definition.

ALTERNATIVE FORMS OF DEFINITION

There are various ways of expressing the definition of a problem. When we give a general but precise description of the problem we are defining it in the best way for communication to other people. The method of stating the objective and the obstacle may be called 'definition for strategy', because it points the way to possible strategic approaches. When we need to draw attention to possible methods of solution, we customarily use the form 'how to ...', such as 'how to get into a locked car without a key'. This form, which may be called 'definition for method', has particular relevance to the tactics to be employed in constructing courses of action and implementation.

STAGE-TYPE PROBLEMS

It is unusual to find a problem which requires an equal amount of attention to be paid to each one of its stages.

Rather, the normal state of affairs is that a problem arises or is posed in such a way as to give particular emphasis to one of the five stages. For instance, the formulation of the problem may be the main issue. This may arise when objectives are not clear or are in conflict, or when a vague awareness of difficulty or impending trouble needs to be clarified. Or a problem may be primarily one of interpretation. We may have our objectives clear but find it difficult to understand something, such as why something has gone wrong or what is the significance of a message or a person's behaviour. Then there are creative problems, such as how to accomplish something or how to meet a need. Decision-making problems are a very obvious type—such as where to go for a holiday, what to spend our money on, what food to buy for the weekend, or what colour to paint the bathroom—bearing in mind, however, that it is the element of choice and commitment that we are thinking of here and not the proposing of courses of action, which belongs to the constructive stage. Implementation problems are also a distinct type. They are concerned with getting things done, such as how to get one's proposals accepted, how to get results, how to avoid making mistakes, and so on.

A direct benefit of adopting an approach to problem-solving based on stages is that it provides a framework for the rapid and accurate identification of types of problems and helps in their diagnosis, enabling us to choose appropriate methods for dealing with each type. It is useful to consider whether the problem we are working on appears to be a formulation-type problem, an interpretation-type problem, a construction-type problem, a decision-making-type problem or an implementation-type problem. This will help to clarify our thoughts and speed up the problem-solving process by bringing quickly to mind useful proposals relating to the stage with which the problem has been identified, such as the principles and methods described in the respective chapters of this book.

At first sight this argument may appear to be slightly paradoxical because, for example, a formulation-type problem may not be recognizable until it has been formulated. But if this should happen, the formulation which would then be required would be a re-formulation—one which would be deeper or broader than the original formulation.

SUMMARY

Here is a summary of the main points in this chapter, expressed as a check-list of advice on the formulation of problems.

1. Be alert and vigilant for signs of trouble.
2. Become an enthusiast at problem-solving.
3. Become an expert in your own subject.
4. Learn to react appropriately to the various types of problem-situations.
5. When problems occur in writing, solve them by simplifying the task.
6. Identify the problem by asking questions.
7. Define the problem by specifying the objective and the obstacle.
8. Check that the definition of the problem is complete and adequate by asking further questions.
9. Remember the mnemonic $P = O + O$.

EXERCISES

1. Identify and define the following problems by stating the objective and the obstacle which is apparently preventing it from being reached.
   (a) Our business competitors are presumably developing new products and markets.
   (b) An acquaintance frequently behaves in an offensive manner towards us, which, to say the least of it, is disconcerting.
   (c) We suspect that there may be dry rot in our house.
   (d) Someone has a bad habit.
2. The 'too-too' situation occurs when a big project associated with our interests is being planned and we have ideas that we think ought to be incorporated, but we are told either that it is too early for such details to be considered or else that it is too late to do anything about them. How can we

avoid the pitfall of the 'too-too' situation? Define the problem first before making your recommendations.

3. When is the best time to buy Christmas presents? Define the problems involved before committing yourself to an answer.

4. Tomorrow, when you plan your day's work, consider each task in turn and ask yourself, 'Is that really essential? Will that really contribute to my objective?'

5. A motorist's engine boils over on a journey. He has to stop and find a supply of water to replace what has been lost. What could have been done to deal with the problem much earlier and with less effort?

6. Think about some problem which will face you in the future, either at work or at home, define it carefully and make some preliminary plan as to what you intend to do about it.

Stage 2

INTERPRETING THE PROBLEM

5

Understanding
and Interpretation

The previous chapter dealt with recognizing the existence of
the problem, making sure that we have the right problem, and
knowing exactly what problem it is. Now we come to the
second stage, the purpose of which is to take us to a position
where we have a clear understanding of the situation in which
the problem has arisen. The reason why this stage is necessary
is quite simple. The mind has to take proper account of all the
important information about the problem if it is to provide
us with a useful solution. It will not be able to do this unless
all the important information is correctly interpreted and
understood.

The truth of this assertion is fairly obvious and can be seen
even more clearly if we consider its converse. If we cannot
interpret and understand the problem-situation correctly the
only hope of hitting upon a satisfactory solution will be by an
extraordinary stroke of good luck! Understanding is achieved
through interpretation by implanting the essential features of
the problem-situation in the solver's mind in circumstances
which permit him to perceive their inter-relationships. It
depends upon the discovery and identification of the relevant
features and how they are related, and on the construction of
what may be called a model of the problem-situation in the
mind which interprets the circumstances of the problem as an
understandable pattern.

In some problems the process of detecting, identifying, and defining a problem correctly is sufficient to show the direction in which the solution lies. A practical example of this arose during the study of a system of aircraft maintenance, where there were seen to be difficulties with the complexity of paperwork used in the clerical part of the system. When some careful thought was given to the identification and definition of this problem it was realized that neither the objective nor the obstacle was the paperwork itself. The objective was the efficient maintenance of the fleet of aircraft and the obstacle was a lack of staff to keep proper records of maintenance work. Once the problem had been defined in these terms the appropriate course of action was obvious—get more staff! The manager concerned, then being quite clear about what was needed, asked for the extra staff and persisted until the request was granted, arguing that the extra costs would be balanced by increased effectiveness. When the staff were found and put to work the difficulties disappeared and the problem was solved.

The process of clarifying this problem until it could be correctly defined produced sufficient understanding for it to be solved without further investigation. But in very many cases, especially the more difficult or more complicated ones, further study is required to reach an understanding which is deep and thorough enough to lead to the construction of sound courses of action.

In Chapter 4 an example was given of defining a problem concerned with the weighing of large aircraft. When some people were trying to solve it they found difficulty in making progress. The reason was not only that the problem was difficult to define properly, but also that they had not paused to consider what weighing really means. They were overlooking many possibilities, such as new methods of weighing, because they had not appreciated the need to understand the problem-situation before trying to devise a solution. They had failed to realize the significance of the component parts of the problem.

OBSTACLES TO CORRECT INTERPRETATION

Interpretation is often a difficult enough problem in itself and there are many possible obstacles that may stand in the way of it. These can be classified in three groups, external circumstances, mental blocks, and bad habits of thought. The purpose of describing them here is to point out that such adverse influences exist and to give some suggestions for overcoming them.

EXTERNAL CIRCUMSTANCES

Our ability to think clearly and effectively is dependent to some extent on the circumstances in which we work. For most people, work which involves noise, interruptions or distractions is not conducive to sound thinking. On the contrary, they prefer peace and quiet in which to think things out properly. The pressure of work affects people differently, some preferring to work under greater pressure than others, but for each of us there is an optimal pressure of work. The effect of insufficient work is to deprive us of stimulation. Too much work can cause us to flit from one problem to another and work superficially, or at worst, to become confused and distressed. Similar effects are produced by the amount of variety in our work. Monotonous work is boring and uninspiring. Excess of variety causes us to fritter our efforts away and lose concentration, but in-between there is an amount of variety that suits us best.

The action we must take is very much alike in all of these instances. We must find out what are the conditions in which we can do our best thinking and make sure that we get them when the need arises. If we need peace and quiet we may have to go away to a place where they can be found. In the office, for example, one way to create the effect of a more peaceful environment is to get up from the desk and take our work over to a comfortable chair. Sometimes the understanding of a difficult point will come more easily if we get up and walk about for a minute or two.

Alternatively, we may have to re-organize the work so that thinking can be done at more suitable places or times. It may be possible to arrange matters so that the practical parts of the work are done in one place, and the problem-solving is done elsewhere but near enough to allow quick consultations between the groups of people concerned when the need arises.

BLOCKS TO INTERPRETATION AND HOW TO OVERCOME THEM

In relation to creative thought, a subject we shall be dealing with in a later chapter, several authors, notably S. Parnes, have drawn our attention to what they call 'blocks'. There are also blocks which interfere with our ability to do the analytical thinking that is necessary to reach a proper interpretation of the problems we are trying to solve. Three types of block have been identified, emotional, perceptual, and cultural.

An emotional block is an emotional reaction to a problem-situation which prevents us from taking a cool analytical look at it. If we are emotionally disturbed we cannot see the problem objectively. If we are very upset we may not be able to think clearly at all. If we are having a discussion with someone and they make us angry we are unlikely to be able to understand what they are really trying to say. If we are talking to somebody and there is something about him that attracts us towards him or that offends us, our interpretation of everything he says or does is likely to be coloured by our emotional reactions. If we are deeply disturbed, for example, as we might be when driving to visit a very sick friend in hospital or on the way home from a funeral, we can be so blocked by emotion that our minds become completely closed to some of the problem-situations arising on the road and we then run a serious risk of causing an accident.

A perceptual block is a limitation or condition which we think is really there but which exists only in our imagination. If, for example, a policeman finds a man staggering about helplessly and smelling strongly of drink, it is possible that he may assume the man to be drunk. This may cause him to fail to discover that the man is suffering from concussion due to a head injury. A perceptual block caused a hold-up for a long time during the period when inter-continental ballistic missiles were first being developed. In this problem the objective was to design a missile that would reach its target in a fully operational condition, and the obstacle was that the heat generated by its passage through the atmosphere would be likely to damage it severely. Everybody had assumed that missiles ought to be pointed or streamlined at the front end, but this belief was false. Eventually a man named H. Julian Allen realized that a blunt nose would absorb heat more slowly than a pointed one, and the problem was then quickly solved.

A cultural block is really a special type of perceptual block, where our perceptions are biased because of the way we have been brought up to regard the things we see around us. For instance, some managers who have been trained in authoritarian institutions like the armed forces find it difficult to understand systems of management which depend upon a more democratic type of approach. Some older people who have been brought up to believe that long hair is an indication of untidiness and inefficiency find it difficult to understand that long-haired men of today can be both orderly and efficient.

The best thing we can do to avoid the harmful effects of blocks to interpretation is to find out which kinds of blocks affect us. This we can do most readily by looking back over our processes of thought whenever we notice that we have not correctly understood a problem-situation, in order to find out why we went wrong. When we have identified a block to which we are susceptible we can mentally prepare ourselves by an effort of will to prevent it from happening again the next time we have to deal with a problem in similar circumstances.

Another thing we can do to avoid mental blocks is to try to take a more detached or impersonal view of our problems. This can be done by restating the definition of a problem, after it has been put in terms of objective and obstacle, in such a way as to include ourselves as the problem-solver in the definition. A way to achieve this is to distinguish two states of affairs, the present state where we are in the problem-situation and the state that will exist once we have reached the objective. As the method needs to be applicable to any situation, it is helpful to give an abstract name to each state, calling the former 'State A' and the latter 'State B'. If we apply this form of definition to the example given in Chapter 2, where the way to work has been blocked by a fallen tree, State A is the situation where my objective is to get to work, but I am prevented by the obstacle of a fallen tree on the road. This kind of definition does not try to say any more about State A. It does not mention the fact that there are no houses nearby, or that I am in a hurry to get to work, etc. All such information, useful or otherwise, is summed up in the expression 'State A', and there is no need to say any more at this preliminary stage. I know also that I wish to get to State B, which is the normal situation that prevails when I get to work safely at the proper time.

The existence of blocks is not a recent discovery, for as long ago as the thirteenth century Roger Bacon was saying more-or-less the same thing. 'There are four stumbling blocks to the way of arriving at knowledge—authority, habit, appearances as they present themselves to the eye, and concealment of ignorance combined with ostentation of knowledge, . . . and we must not use the triple argument; that is to say, this has been laid down, this has been usual, this has been common, therefore it is to be held by. For the very opposite conclusion does much better follow from the premises.'

BAD HABITS AND ATTITUDES

In this section we shall discuss talkativeness, solution-mindedness and superficiality. Talkativeness, like many other faults, is more easily recognized and more readily condemned in other people than in ourselves, but it is a common cause of inefficiency in problem-solving. We have all met the person who says that he cannot really spare the time to discuss our problem because he is so very busy and has always so many pressing problems of his own to deal with. When we meet him, however, he subjects us to a barrage of complaints and self-justifying explanations which use up nearly all of the time available and effectively prevent any profitable use of the occasion.

What can we do to combat this difficulty? If we are too talkative ourselves we can watch other people's expressions for signs of impatience and learn to pause frequently to give them a chance to think and to speak. When it is a matter of controlling the garrulity of other people there are several different courses of action that we may take. Ultimately, we can always interrupt politely or brusquely as appropriate by means of various kinds of question, or by cutting in with a remark to act as a starting point for a contribution of our own. But before it comes to that there are other ways of controlling the other person's flow of talk by means of changes in our own posture, facial expression, and gesture. In his book *The Psychology of Interpersonal Behaviour*, Michael Argyle gives a great deal of interesting information from various researches on this subject.

SOLUTION-MINDEDNESS

Some people are so eager to achieve results that they start to think about possible solutions to each problem they meet before they have found out what the problem really means. As well as being solution-minded they are inclined to make their decisions prematurely as well. Often the range of courses of action they are prepared to consider is limited to those they have successfully carried out in the past in similar circumstances. If we are like this ourselves, it will help if we can learn to move more deliberately in our progress from stage to stage when trying to solve difficult problems. We may have to reconsider our ideas from time to time and be prepared to repeat earlier stages. If, however, it is the other fellow who is solution-minded, he may be one of those people who are not so easily persuaded by a reasoned argument alone but are more easily convinced of the value of a new idea by a dramatic or very neat presentation. If we can show him our analysis of the problem in a sufficiently striking manner, he may be able to get back into the understanding stage from which he may then be able to move forward in a more open-minded and imaginative fashion.

Here is an example of an investigation which started off in the wrong direction because of 'solution-mindedness'. Several years ago I was asked to find out the best way to use an extra radio-frequency channel that had been allotted to an airline by the Post Office. This radio-frequency had been requested in order to improve communications between the station control office, responsible for co-ordinating all the various activities involved in the preparation of aeroplanes for passenger and cargo flights, and the men who supervised the work going on in each separate aeroplane. In analysing this problem it was necessary to find out what was meant by 'communications' in this context. 'Communications' turned out to be a very complicated system for exchanging information between a large number of different people in different places, but all of the communications had to pass by way of one or other of two 'controllers' on duty in the station control office. It quickly became apparent that the controllers were placed at a 'bottleneck' in the information system, and no amount of extra radio-frequencies or any other means of communicating with other people would have been able to help them in the slightest. The objective that had been set in the beginning, which was to find out the best way to use an extra radio-frequency, was a false objective. It was not really needed at all. What was needed was a way to reduce the workload of the two controllers, so as to enable them to handle a greater number of messages than they were able to cope with before. Once this more realistic objective had been identified, it did not take long to find a way of solving the problem. A better way of sharing the task between the two controllers was found and this produced the desired effect. This example shows clearly the danger of looking for a solution before the inner workings of the situation are fully understood.

SUPERFICIALITY

The bad habit of dealing with problems at a superficial level can stem from several causes. Sometimes it is the result of long experience of having to work hurriedly or having to cope with too wide a variety of problems. Sometimes it is an inborn or at least ingrained mental characteristic, linked in some cases with an inability to think in the abstract and to generalize. It is not merely a matter of limited mental ability because there are some very intelligent people who have a dislike of deep and prolonged mental work. They are often men of action who like to make a decision quickly so that they can do something of practical use as soon as possible.

Superficiality of thought is not easy to overcome. Perhaps the most helpful approach to it is to encourage the person concerned to analyse the problem systematically for a while and as soon as he becomes tired or impatient, to stop and change to some other kind of activity. Another approach is to encourage him by showing him good examples of what can be achieved when we do persevere long enough. To immerse ourselves deeply in the complications and under-currents of some problems may require a kind of courage, which is different from the courage required to go all out for the objective in one heroic leap. This can be developed like the courage of an athlete, by experiencing a series of tests in situations of gradually increasing difficulty, with the method-ical approach of problem-solving as a reassuring guide. The simple rules that we shall be advocating for the study of problem-situations are like a life-line. If we follow them we shall get across with the least possible difficulty, but if we ignore them we may flounder about for a long time before making any worthwhile progress.

SUMMARY

We have been discussing in this chapter the need to make sure that we understand the situation of a problem before we start to put forward ideas for its solution. Understanding can be made easy or difficult by the circumstances in which we work and can be prejudiced by various emotional, perceptual, and cultural blocks, and other attitudes. All of these are highly individual influences but the way to overcome them is basically similar. If we study our own successes and failures we shall see which conditions suit us best and which weak-nesses we are most prone to. This knowledge will show us where we need to develop better practices and better habits of thought.

EXERCISES

1. Consider the environment in which you are reading now. Is it ideal for the purpose? Try to improve it, or go and read for a while in another place and compare it for

suitability with where you are now. If this makes a difference, what is the reason for it?

2. Write down a word or two to describe a mistake or error that you made recently. What was the cause of it? Could it be attributed to an emotional, perceptual, or cultural block? If so, how could you avoid making a similar mistake or error in the future?

3. Consider any problem that you are trying to solve. Define it in terms of State A, where you are now, and State B, where you are trying to get to. Are your own actions or attitudes a part of the problem? If so, can you modify them and thereby reduce the severity of the problem?

4. Do you ever ask people for advice about your problems? Do people ever come to you for advice? In either case, who does most of the talking? Is this right? If not, what can you do to control the situation? Are there some people who don't really want to solve their problems?

5. When people say, 'Let's stop all this talking and do something', they may be judging the situation correctly or incorrectly, depending upon whether the talking is necessary or not. How can we tell how much talking is necessary?

6. When someone we are working with is going ahead too fast with an ill-considered plan of action, what can we do to control the situation?

7. How can we train ourselves to think carefully?

8. Can a computer solve a person's problem? If this is partially correct, what kinds of problem can a computer solve and not solve?

6

The Use of Models

We have already referred to the concept of a model. A model is a representation of a situation, system or thing. It gives shape, structure, and pattern to our ideas and can be made of something that will hold our ideas in a lasting form. Understanding, we said, depends on the ability to construct a model of the situation in the mind. If we want to build up a mental model of some situation and we are clever enough, we can think it all out by pure and unaided brain-power. But if we are not so clever it is very useful to have some kind of external model, equivalent in some way to our thoughts, to look at and to think about. It is an advantage to be able to build such a model in step with the advances made during the thinking process, so that it is available as a record of where we have got to at any stage.

In a very complicated situation, a model to look at and think about is essential for holding and displaying all the important features of the situation and their relationships, and without one our mind is as helpless as an orchestra with no score to play from.

WORDS AS MODELS

The nearest kind of model to the purely mental model is the model constructed of words. Words are our foremost means for handling ideas. We have a good word for nearly everything and if we find a need for a new word we can invent one.

65

Words are versatile because they can be thought about, conveyed from person to person or recorded for an indefinite period. They are not without disadvantages, however, because they can tempt us to think in blinkers and fail to see each other's meaning, especially when we forget that we are dealing with abstractions from reality and start talking about them as if they were things.

The way we use words is a fascinating field of study in itself. The old phrase 'spinning a yarn' describes it well, reflecting the fact that the utterance of words is a process of pulling out ideas and marshalling them into a flowing thread of discourse. Word-spinning is a perfect creative process because no matter how many words are produced the source of supply is never depleted. On the contrary, the capacity to produce words always increases with practice.

The most common kind of word-model is a description in prose of some situation. We all make such models frequently in conversation and in writing, but we do not all have the same level of skill in knowing what to put in the description and how to express it. This skill can be developed by the regular application of problem-solving methods to difficulties which we meet in writing and composition.

Prose has the advantage of being a familiar and acceptable vehicle for carrying information about a situation, but it has some disadvantages in problem-solving work. It comes in highly organized pieces which are not easy to alter or to expand. If we try to change a piece of writing it gets into a messy state very easily. It is easier to start building up a word-model from separate words rather than from whole pieces of prose. If we make a list of words that represent various ideas we have in mind, this can be re-arranged at any time. Similarly, short notes in abbreviated form are much more flexible and useful at first than whole sentences or paragraphs. Prose follows essentially a linear or serial process, with the words strung in a row like a necklace, and it is best suited to the description of situations which can be represented easily by a long chain of ideas. The majority of situations in which we are interested and which give rise to our problems are many-sided, and so we need to find many-sided ways of describing them.

Practical Examples of Words as Models

The simplest way to represent a situation in words is to make a list of its main features. This is what we do, for example, when making a list of things to take on a holiday; a list of food and drink needed for a party, a list of people to invite to a dinner, or a list of jobs to be done. A list can be given structure by re-writing it in a meaningful sequence or putting its items into groups. The list of things to take on a holiday might be grouped so as to keep clothes, sports gear, and other items separate. The list of jobs might be put into order of priority. These examples are of a kind where the items are very definite like common objects, people, and jobs. The same method of listing and grouping can also be applied to more abstract ideas that we may be trying to record, such as the subjects to be discussed at a meeting or the influences which may be aggravating a difficult situation.

An alternative to grouping the items within a single list is to divide the list into several columns, one for each different sort of item. This has the advantage of bringing the differences out more clearly and making the grouping more obvious. It also makes the task of drawing up the list easier because it provides a choice of places in which to write each new item as it is added to the list.

When it is possible to sub-divide each of the columns into similar parts we have the opportunity to draw up a table or cross-classification. This does not happen very often but it does occur in constructing timetables, programmes, and statistical tables such as for comparing the characteristics of different people, countries, factories, machines, etc. An example familiar to motorists is the table of lubricants often included in motor-car handbooks, where for each major operating unit of a car the recommended lubricants of various manufacturers are listed.

CHAIN DIAGRAMS

One of the most useful ways of using the power of words in modelling problem-situations is to set out the words in different places and link them up with lines to form a chain diagram. This is often an extremely clear, economical and stimulating way of bringing out the essentials of a problem, either for the purpose of analysis or for communicating a point of view to other people. The family tree is a well-known and rather formal example of this type of device.

Some problems involve several elements which it is desirable to recognize and to keep distinct from each other. Suppose we are trying to solve a problem concerned with the cost of

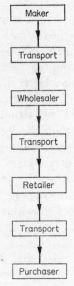

FIGURE 4.   A chain diagram for furniture supply

furniture. It may be helpful to visualize the chain of supply by drawing a diagram as shown in Figure 4.

In this case the diagram will help us to understand where the components of cost come from and how they build up from the initial cost to the maker, to the final cost to the consumer. This, like Figure 3 (p. 13) in Chapter 2, has been shown as a simple chain of items, but figures of this kind can equally well be branched, folded, looped, etc., to show many different kinds of relationship between the elements. Arrows showing the direction of flow of information, goods, or money can be incorporated, and so can numbers, which add a quantitative dimension. Figure 5 shows a model of the main sources from which a manager's daily supply of work-problems might come to him for attention.

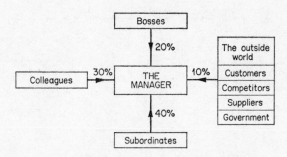

FIGURE 5.   Possible sources of a manager's problems

In Chapter 13 the use in decision-making of the branched form of chain diagram called a tree-diagram, will be described in detail.

Fault-tree Diagrams

It was shown by H. A. Watson of the Bell Telephone Laboratories that tree diagrams have a useful application to the study of faults in systems. Figure 6 (p. 70) is a fault-tree diagram to illustrate the possible causes of not receiving daily newspapers at home. Items in rectangles are events which have known causes. Items in circles are events which are not intended to be analysed further. The small circles are 'logic gates', all of which in this example are 'or' gates, which means that any one of the events arrowed into a small circle will be sufficient to cause the fault shown in the rectangle above. If we have enough information about the probabilities of occurrence, it is possible to calculate the relative importance of the various branches of the diagram in causing the event at the top, and to show whether or not there are any possible ways of simplifying the diagram.

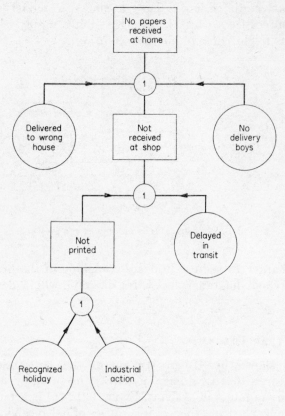

FIGURE 6.   A fault-tree for non-delivery of newspapers

MEANS/ENDS BLOCK DIAGRAMS

A common cause of difficulty in understanding a complex problem is the confusion which arises when people fail to distinguish between means and ends. This often occurs when there is a set of rules and a formal procedure for doing something and it is not readily apparent why some things have to be done and others have not to be done.

A means/ends block diagram can be drawn to show which features of the system are ultimate ends or objectives and which are merely means to those ends. Consider, for example, the procedure that we have to go through at a public swimming bath. We buy a ticket, we collect a clothes basket, we deposit the basket in a store, we pass through a shower or foot-bath, and finally we bathe. Why do we do all this? What purpose

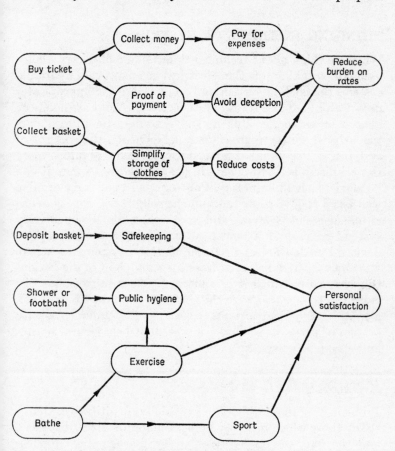

FIGURE 7.   A means/ends block diagram—swimming bath procedure

do these procedures serve? Let us take them one at a time. We buy a ticket so that the authorities can collect money to pay for their expenses and reduce the burden on the rate-payers. The ticket is proof of payment. Why do we need proof? To avoid deception. Why do we need to avoid deception? Again, to reduce the burden on the rate-payers.

In a similar fashion the purposes of the other procedures can
be thought out, and all can be shown in a diagram such as
in Figure 7 (p. 71). The procedures start at the left and the
arrows lead on to the more ultimate objectives on the right.

THINKING IN TERMS OF SYSTEMS

When we think about technical things like motor-cars we are
used to speaking of the electrical system, the hydraulic
system, the cooling system and so on. Here the appropriate-
ness of thinking in terms of systems is so obvious as to appear
almost unavoidable. But in less deterministic things, particularly where there are human components, the concept of
systems is less familiar and its application requires more
mental discipline. However, there are situations where it can
be particularly illuminating. For example, a colleague of mine
was asked to give some talks on the subjects of 'the school as
a management system' and 'the school as a supervisory
system' as part of a course of training for school teachers
devised by Alan Paisey, in which the total system of a school
was analysed and discussed from the standpoint of the various
sub-systems of which it is composed. Other sub-systems discussed in this course were the school as a production system,
a system of human groups, a system of communications, a
system of needs satisfaction, a system of behavioural norms,
and an adaptive system.

MATHEMATICAL MODELS

Problem-situations which are essentially quantitative, that is
to say those which involve numbers, amounts, sizes, distances,
and the like, can be represented by mathematical models.
Mathematical models have many advantages and are often,
though not always, more effective than other kinds of models.
It is an advantage to know something about their possibilities
and to be able to judge whether a mathematical model could
be helpful in trying to understand a given problem-situation.
    For those who like mathematical work there are many
books on applied mathematics and operational research which
explain fully how mathematical techniques can be used in

problem-solving. Our purpose in this section is not to go into such detail but just to explain what mathematical models are and how they can be helpful.

Let us consider some simple practical problems of everyday life to show that there is nothing unfamiliar about the principle of applying mathematics in quantitative situations. Take, for example, the problem of sowing a lawn with seed. The experts have already worked out and tested the models we need. Some kinds of grass seed produce the best results when sown at the rate of 50 grams per square metre. To find out how many kilos of seed we need for our lawn we have to calculate the area of the lawn in square metres, multiply by 50 and then convert from grams to kilos. We have been given a ready-made mathematical model and we know how to use it to solve a certain kind of problem.

Suppose we are going to make a journey by air. We know the departure time of the flight and we wish to know at what time we ought to be ready to leave home to start the journey. There are various time allowances that we may need to make. Let us assume for the purpose of this example that they are as shown in the following table.

Check-in period	40 mins
Park car	15 mins
Road journey	30 mins
Allowance for delays in traffic	15 mins
Total	1 hr 40 mins

What we have done is to construct a model in mathematical terms of the important aspects of the problem of timing our journey and used it to obtain an understanding of the situation. We have interpreted the problem mathematically.

In similar ways we are familiar with the application of mathematical ideas to such problems as working out the time it takes to roast a turkey, at so much plus so much per pound, the number of words to go into a speech at so many per minute, the duration of a journey by underground at two minutes per station, or the cost of carpeting a room at so much per square yard. These employ mathematical models of the simplest possible order. A little more complication is required to deal mathematically with such problems as choosing the size of a fuse for an electrical appliance, for converting degrees fahrenheit to degrees centigrade, for working out interest on loans and mortgages, for calculating the required thickness of a rope to take a given load, or for calculating the dimensions of a beam to support part of a building, and so on.

At the other extreme we are familiar with what has been achieved by the use of some of the most complicated of mathematical models, in spite of the fact that not many of us appreciate that they have been used, let alone understand them. The astonishing events of the astronautical programmes of the USA and the USSR are spectacular examples in this category. It seems almost incredible that it is possible to calculate with a high degree of accuracy where and when men will land on the surface of the moon or the earth after several days of travel in the unexplored distances of space, yet this can be and has been consistently done.

A much older example is the phenomenon of radio transmission. The fact that radio waves can be generated and propagated through space was not found out by accident. It was discovered as a mathematical consequence of the properties of the elementary particles of matter, and was predicted as a possibility years before practical methods of achieving it were developed. Such marvels are near the limit of human comprehension but they can, nevertheless, serve as an example of the kinds of achievement that are possible and hence provide a source of encouragement to our intellectual efforts.

How Mathematical Models are Useful

It may be easier to appreciate the meaning and value of mathematical models if we give some attention to the various functions that they can perform. At the most simple level a mathematical model is a means of quantifying something that is not itself a quantity. A flock of sheep becomes a number of sheep once its members have been counted. One of the ancient methods of doing this before numbers became widely used was for the shepherd to take a pocketful of pebbles, one for each sheep in the flock, so that he could find out at any time whether any of them had strayed or become lost; hence our word 'calculate' which literally means to use pebbles. The set of pebbles represented the flock of sheep and acted as a quantitative model of it.

Similarly, a set of marks obtained in an examination is a model of the capabilities of the examinees and a means of comparing them. We judge the validity of the examination by the accuracy with which we believe the marks represent the capabilities of the examinees.

A mathematical model can be very useful in helping us to understand a problem. Take, for example, the problem of designing braking systems for vehicles. The main objective is to be able to bring a vehicle travelling at high speed safely to a halt. From calculus we know that the deceleration of a vehicle moving initially at a given velocity and coming to rest over a given distance at a constant rate of deceleration is proportional to the square of the velocity divided by the distance. From Newton's second law of motion we know that the braking force required to produce a deceleration is proportional to the mass of the vehicle multiplied by the deceleration. Therefore we can deduce that the braking force required is proportional to the mass of the vehicle multiplied by the square of the velocity and divided by the stopping distance. In the concise language of algebra this can be stated as $F \propto mv^2/d$. This model shows that the most important factor is the velocity because it is the only one whose effect is squared. A vehicle going at twice a given velocity would require four times the braking force to stop in the same distance.

Models of any kind are useful as instruments of communication, because they help other people to reach the same understanding of a situation as we do ourselves. In some kinds of communication problem the message is more telling if it is put over in quantitative terms. For example, if in a business most of the employees are of a similar age, the time will come when all the staff in important positions are due to retire and there will be nobody with the right qualifications and experience ready to succeed them. It may be that until this time comes no-one will take any positive step to remedy the situation, even though several persons in the senior ranks may be vaguely aware of the position and the dangers involved. However, it only requires some simple calculations to be able to show vividly by means of charts and diagrams how the situation is deteriorating year by year and what should be done to put things right again. Information in quantitative form can be more dramatic and convincing to those in authority than unquantified opinion.

A mathematical model can enable us to calculate the consequences of variations that may occur in the problem-situation in order, for example, to forecast what will happen in the future. A mathematical model can also be used to test various alternative possibilities or to prove or disprove a point being argued. Models can be constructed to deal with systems having large numbers of elements with complex relationships, or to cope with uncertainty and risk, to calculate with very large quantities or very small, and to represent a wide variety of special relationships beyond those that we learn about in simple arithmetic, algebra, and geometry.

A specially interesting and useful feature of mathematical models is their adaptability, by which it can be possible to use the same basic model to fit a range of different problem-situations. Thus, we know from Pythagoras's theorem that in any right-angled triangle on a flat surface, no matter what its size, if we call the lengths of the two sides forming the right-angle a and b, and the third side c, then in all circumstances $a^2 + b^2 = c^2$. Speaking much more generally, we know that the geometrical properties of a given class of triangle are always the same regardless of their actual sizes and proportions. Another familiar example refers to mathematical series, such as 1 2 3 4 5 . . . or 2 4 6 8 . . . or 10 20 30 40 . . . or 2 4 8 16 . . . etc. The formulae that have been worked out for solving problems involving series like these can be used successfully over and over again, as long as we obey the rules for applying them to particular circumstances. What is more, the properties of mathematical series may be recognized in situations in which we would not perhaps anticipate finding them, such as things which are interesting to look at like a cactus, a ram's horn, or a snail's shell.

Another example of versatility among mathematical models

is shown in the type of problem-situation where something of the nature of a queue builds up. It does not matter in the least what the queue consists of or what it is queueing up for. It can be made of people at a bus stop, at a post-office counter, or in a cafeteria. It can be of motor-cars waiting to be painted, to be repaired, or to pass the traffic lights. It can be cows waiting to be milked or telephone calls waiting to be answered. All such queueing situations have similar mathematical properties, so that a mathematician can usually find a model which will fit and enable him to predict how the system will behave.

Many non-mathematicians have the ability to learn to use mathematical methods when they really need to, but the majority will not do so because of their attitudes towards the subject; unfortunately they will be too easily put off by their distaste for it, which is another example of a cultural block. What they ought to do, perhaps, is to learn to recognize an opportunity for using the mathematical approach and when one turns up they can then ask a mathematician to give them help or advice, which is much better than reverting to subjective methods of tackling the quantitative kind of problem.

CLASSIFICATION

Certain kinds of complex problem can be simplified by classification. This is particularly true when there are elements of the problem which are similar in some respects but different in others. Whenever we ask a question and the reply is, 'It all depends', we can be fairly sure that there is a need for classification. Whenever we notice that a particular action is easy to do well in some circumstances but difficult in others, it is also likely that the problem will be understood better if we define the circumstances and make a classification of them. It has long been recognized that the process of classification is an important stage in the work of scientists as, for example, in biology, geology, and chemistry.

Whenever we think we are in one of these 'it all depends' situations we can explore it by asking, 'Does this situation occur in one way only, or are there several different ways?' If there are several, 'What are they?' The next thing we can do is to write the different kinds down in a list.

For example, I used to receive frequent requests at work for advice and help from people who were not employees of the company. The problem was to know what to do about it. Well, it all depended on what sort of people they were and what they wanted. This looked like a classification problem. What were the different kinds of people and the kinds of help that they wanted? Here is my analysis of the situation.

Enquirers	*Requests*
Research workers	Funds and facilities
Young people (*a*) complete strangers	Financial support for training or education
(*b*) with connections	Information
Consultants	Assignments
	Information
Salesmen	Orders
Various acquaintances	References
Ex-service men	Employment
Educational specialists	Visits
	Nominations for their courses

It became apparent from this analysis that there were many different possible combinations of enquirers and requests, but they were not unmanageable because some of the classes could be grouped together and there was a tendency for requests to be specific to the particular class of enquirers who made them. I then saw that a simple principle or rule could be laid down for dealing with each class of request, which is how I solved the problem. For instance, I had previously prepared leaflets explaining the scheme that we operated for the financial support of research students. If there were funds remaining in the research budget I sent a leaflet to anyone enquiring for support for a research project that looked suitable, on the principle of first come, first served. If there were no funds left or if the research project was not suitable I sent a standard letter to say so. Requests for employment from ex-service men were acknowledged and then passed to another department which had authority to take appropriate action. For references

I developed a standard formula which simplified the task of writing them without losing the flexibility which is required to do justice to the talents of individuals.

Here is another example. A manager decided to start a series of regular meetings with his staff in order to improve communications with them. After drawing up some preliminary suggestions he realized that he needed to hold different kinds of meetings for different purposes. He then attempted to classify these purposes, with the following results.

Purposes

1. To inform staff about new policies.
2. To improve morale.
3. To give instructions.
4. To gather advice and news.
5. To solve problems.

Having made this analysis, he proceeded to choose a suitable form of communications for each purpose, viz.:

Purpose	*Form of Communication*
1. Policies	By written statement.
2. Morale	By informal talks to small groups.
3. Instructions	Through normal organizational channels.
4. Advice and news	Through normal organizational channels and short weekly meetings.
5. Problems	In working parties and normal working groups.

The most satisfactory classifications are exhaustive, in that they cover all eventualities and there is a place for every example that might come up. However, this is not always easy to arrange because we may not be able to consider enough examples to be aware of the full range of possibilities. We should therefore be careful to avoid drawing any inferences which depend upon the assumption that our classification is complete, unless we are sure that it is.

STANDARD MODELS

Some types of problem-situation are so common and general that models describing them can be used over and over again. We have noted this aspect of some mathematical models, but it applies to other kinds as well. These are the most valuable of models because of their wide applicability and because we may learn by repeated experience to use them more and more skilfully. In Chapter 3 we touched on some common types of recognizable problem such as control problems, personal differences, searching, and problems caused by ambiguity. As an example of how a common type of problem can be modelled we shall now consider the communication type of problem, which perhaps is the most common of all.

COMMUNICATION PROBLEMS

Whenever we have a situation where something passes or ought to pass from one person to another, any problem that arises can be studied as a communication problem and nearly all communication problems have the same essential features connected by the same relationships. The essential features are as in the table below, and the predominant relationship between them is that they follow in a logical sequence.

We can demonstrate the properties of this list by applying it to realistic situations in which communication is involved. In Table 1 (p. 81) we have two examples, one of a manager ordering a book by post and the other of the Prime Minister making a speech on television.

The way to use the model is to take any problem situation which is essentially a communication system or which depends upon a communication system, and identify in it as many as possible of the typical elements of a communication system. Each element can then be considered in turn to see whether there is a gap in the system, a blockage, a cause of distortion, or any other apparent fault. The model serves a similar purpose to that of a circuit diagram used by an electrical engineer to help him understand a piece of equipment and find faults which have developed in it. It identifies all the

TABLE 1. A model of the communication process

How we communicate	Examples of communication	
How we communicate		*Examples of communication*
A sender or originator	A manager	The Prime Minister
makes a decision to communicate	decides to send an order	decides to speak to the people
in order to bring about an intended effect	for the supply of a book	to enlist their co-operation in a matter of national importance
and produces a message or thing	and his instructions	and prepares a speech
which is packed or encoded	are typed	which he reads
in a container or code	in a letter	in a television broadcast
which is then dispatched or transmitted	which is sent	which is transmitted
in a vehicle	in an envelope	in a pattern of electro-magnetic waves
via a link, route or channel	by mail	on BBC and ITV frequency channels
and received	and arrives at the booksellers	and collected at the aerials of TV receivers
and unpacked or decoded	and opened	and displayed in sound and vision
and the recipient	and the bookseller	and the people
reacts or responds.	reads it and originates dispatch of the book.	see and hear and react in their various ways.

components and shows how information passes from one point to another.

In electronic communication systems there is a further concept which can be carried over and applied to other kinds of communication system. This is the principle of matching impedances. Energy can most easily flow from one system to another if the impedances of the two systems or appropriate parts of them are similar. In audio equipment, for example, the impedance of a loud-speaker should be similar to the output impedance of the amplifier which feeds it. A mechanical analogy is to be found in the motor-car, where a gear-box is required in order to transform the output of the engine so that it will match the 'impedance' of the transmission system. Extending this to the field of human communication, we can see how it is relevant to the relationship between a speaker and his audience, or a teacher and his pupils. Whoever is the transmitter must deliberately modify his 'output impedance' to match the 'input impedance' of the receiver. In writing this book I must try to use terminology and style which as many as possible of my readers can accept easily and willingly. It is inevitable that some readers will find that it does not match up with their requirements because it is too easy or too difficult for them, or because my style of writing is not what they are used to. This is one reason why people can have better communication when they know each other better. They have had time to find out how to adapt their 'input and output impedances' to each other.

In our attempts to analyse and understand communication problems, we should not forget that human communication systems can convey emotional implications as well as information. The emotional element in a message can go wrong by entering where it is not intended or by failing to arrive at its destination. Emotions are more reliably communicated in a face-to-face situation where gestures and facial expressions, which are also kinds of model, can supplement language and where the response can be observed directly and corrected if a mistake should be made by either party. Written messages, on the other hand, are often misinterpreted because they do not communicate emotions accurately and unambiguously.

THE USE OF CARDS

One of the most effective and versatile methods of presenting a collection of things or ideas for the purpose of analysis, is to write down the name of each item, or a few words describing it, on a small piece of card like a blank visiting card. Each item is then represented by a different word on a card, and the set of cards represents the whole collection of items. For example, let us imagine that we wish to design a method of classifying correspondence for a filing system. If we take a number of cards and write on each the name of a particular type of correspondence that we have to deal with, then we can easily move the cards about on the surface of a table or desk in order to put them together in groups of similar types. By this means we analyse the nature of our correspondence in a very simple fashion.

Similarly, let us imagine that we have received a complicated message and that we are trying to understand what it means so that we can decide what to do about it. We can write a word or phrase on each of a number of cards to represent the main ideas or topics included in the message. We can then put them together in some sort of pattern or sequence which seems to reflect the intention implied in the message. This may enable us to find an interpretation of the message which is both meaningful and plausible.

Another example is where we are planning an investigation. We can use words on cards to represent the different items or topics to be investigated, and we can give structure to them by putting them in an order which will be the most logical or efficient for our purpose.

The use of cards demonstrates how the process of analysis or breaking-down leads to the process of synthesis or building-up. We may use them to analyse the types of books in a library and then build up a system of classification, or to analyse the nature of the work done in a business enterprise and build up an organization chart.

SUMMARY

The message of this chapter is that complex situations are easier to understand when we use models to represent them. The components of models can take many shapes and forms such as words, marks on paper or real things. We have considered several types of diagram suitable for modelling different types of situation and other general approaches such as the use of mathematics and classification.

There are a number of typical classes of problem for which generalized models have already been devised. If we can identify problems by the class of model which is appropriate, and put the model to use, we can quickly overcome many difficulties in interpretation. The skills of recognizing opportunities for modelling and of applying models can only be developed by practice. The benefits of increased understanding will be obtained if we are determined to apply our skills when real problems arise.

EXERCISES

1. A bridge has collapsed into a river. Write down a list of possible events which could have caused this to happen and draw a block diagram to show the logical relationships between them.
2. Take a piece of mechanism, such as a clock or a lawnmower, and draw a diagram (not to scale) to show how it works.
3. In your occupation, how does information come to you, and what do you do with it? Draw a diagram to illustrate the processes involved and the lines of communication.
4. Draw a diagram to depict the flow of goods, packages, and other material in and out of your home.
5. To make tea a number of resources are required, and several systems, such as water and electrical supply, may need to function correctly if we are to achieve a satisfactory result. Draw a fault-tree diagram to show what events and combinations of events could prevent success in making and serving a pot of tea. Use cards or pieces of

paper on which to write down the items needed, and then arrange them in tree-like form and copy the result onto a sheet of paper. Since some of the apparatus, such as saucers, is not essential, use suitable notation to distinguish the essential items from the non-essential.

6. Draw a means/ends block diagram to show why we use the various items and procedures for making a pot of tea that you identified in the exercise above.

7. Make a list of the systems which operate in your home.

8. Express the following relationships as mathematical models, either in words or algebraic symbols.
   (a) The value of a rectangular sheet of postage stamps.
   (b) The time taken to mow a rectangular lawn, ignoring, if you wish, the emptying of the grass-box.
   (c) The length of a shoe-lace for a shoe with a given number of lace-holes.
   (d) The distance one has to walk forwards in going up a flight of stairs.

9. Draw a graph to show the changes in your annual income during your career. What does this tell you? What can you reasonably expect in the future?

10. Take out the contents of your pockets, brief-case or hand-bag. Classify them by placing them in groups of similar kind. Write down a word or two to serve as a name for each group. What does this indicate about you as a person?

11. A tour operator selling package holidays advertises his product on television and a viewer responds by writing off for a holiday brochure and eventually books one of the advertised holidays. Make a list of the entire sequence of events from the beginning to the end of this transaction, following the model of communication given in Table 1 (p. 81).

7

The Technique of Analysis

Although the ability to understand situations depends upon the mental abilities of the problem-solver, there are ways of making sure that we use our capabilities to their fullest extent. A systematic method of analysis is one of these.

The main effect of analysis is to break a problem down into smaller part-problems that are easier to understand and to solve than the whole problem was in its original form. However, there is more to it than taking something to pieces. It is not a destructive process but a creative one, because it involves seeking and finding meaningful relationships which link the pieces together. Consider, for example, chemical analysis. This does not end in the dissociation of a given substance into its constituent elements. On the contrary, it ends in a constructive description of the nature of the substance, expressed in terms appropriate for solving the problem for which the analysis was required.

Similarly, mental analysis of a problem-situation, statement, set of ideas, or system can lead to a constructive description of its essential features. The process of analysis and its outcome are constructive aids to the interpretation of the matter we are considering.

Here are four practical steps to be followed in analysis:

1. Divide the situation or any available information about it into distinguishable parts.

2. Take each part or item by itself and study it until you know enough about it to be able to describe it.
3. State how the parts relate to each other and how they relate together to form the whole situation.
4. Study and describe critically the situation as a whole.

WHAT CAN BE ANALYSED?

Now that we have the tool of analysis ready to use, the next step is to know what to apply it to. But that is not difficult at all. The process can be applied profitably to any of the following:

1. Any definition or description of the problem.
2. The objective.
3. The obstacle.
4. Any other feature or aspect of the situation.

ANALYSIS OF THE OBJECTIVE AND OBSTACLE

Here is a disguised version of an objective that was formulated by a manager and analysed by his staff according to the rules given above.

> 'To examine the likely operational problems arising from a joint operation with ABC Airways at Blankfield airport and estimate probable resultant savings.'

Every word of this objective was examined separately and in most cases a period of discussion was required before an acceptable interpretation could be agreed. Further discussions of the whole idea were needed to make sure that everybody concerned was clear about the full implications of what had seemed at first sight to be a straightforward objective. It was evident that without such careful analysis the manager's intentions would not have been understood properly.

When an obstacle is to be subjected to analysis there are several pertinent questions that may be asked, such as those in the list below. The answers will invariably prove to be a source of useful ideas for the next stage, where we begin to look for ways by which the obstacle might be overcome.

Similar questions may be posed about the objective also, pursuing in greater detail those listed in Chapter 4.

The obstacle—
What is its nature? (Have we any knowledge of this sort of thing?)
What is its origin? (Can it be got rid of the way it came?)
What is its effect? (Can we adapt to it?)
How big is it? (Can we overwhelm it, tolerate it?)
How tractable is it? (Can we draw it away?)
How real is it? (Can we just ignore it?)
How permanent is it? (Can we wait for it to fade away?)

Other features of the problem susceptible to analysis include various principles, constraints or limitations, and various sorts of secondary or lesser objectives and obstacles which may be recognized.

EXAMPLES OF ANALYSIS

Let us take as an exercise the problem about weighing aircraft that we have mentioned on previous occasions. One of the ways of defining it was to say that there were two objectives; to meet the requirements of the law about weighing aircraft and also to avoid weighing the new large aircraft. The obstacle was the fact that these two objectives conflict with each other.

How can we analyse this problem to understand it better and at the same time determine where to start looking for courses of action which may possibly lead us to a solution? First of all, what distinguishable parts are there to this problem? A little thought reveals the following.

1. The law about weighing aircraft.
2. Weighing.
3. The new large aircraft.

To study each of these parts we can ask several fairly obvious questions, separately and in relation to each other.

What exactly is the law about weighing aircraft?
Do we have to obey it?

What does 'weighing' mean, (*a*) legally and (*b*) mechanically?
What methods are possible for weighing aircraft?
Would they all be legal?
What must be done to weigh the new large aircraft?
What exactly are the disadvantages of weighing?
Can they be avoided?
Are they truly not acceptable?

By the time we have found answers to these questions we should have reached a considerable understanding of the situation. We may even begin to see possible ways of solving the problem. If we have not been able to find answers our understanding will be incomplete and it is quite likely that one or more feasible solutions will remain hidden from us.

As to the relations between the parts of the problem, these were already expressed in the definition of the problem, but now we might be able to re-formulate it, saying that the objective is a joint one of meeting the law about the weighing of aircraft and at the same time avoiding the inconvenience normally involved in weighing and the high cost of buying extra weighing machinery. The obstacle of a conflict between the two objectives might be found to be not so difficult to overcome after all. It might be possible to avoid the extra cost by extending the capabilities of the existing equipment, or it might be possible to reduce the inconvenience of the weighing process by re-organizing the procedure by which it is done.

Here is another example taken to a further stage of analysis. Consider this situation. I visit a friend who is an invalid living in a private residential home for elderly people. I enter the building and on my way to my friend's room I am met by a dog carrying a piece of bedroom slipper. The question arises, should I take any notice or should I ignore the dog and his piece of slipper? This is a decision-type problem. My main objective is to do what is best for my friend, and I also have similar but vaguer objectives related to the welfare of any other people associated with this incident. The obstacle is the appearance of the dog, which for the moment leaves me not knowing the best thing to do.

Analysis reveals the following information, which in normal

circumstances would be thought out instantly and privately but for the purpose of showing how this method of analysis works and in the interest of fairness towards dogs, there is no harm in setting it down formally and in detail. We shall see what it looks like to put the results of analysis in the form of a list with various headings.

Parts of the situation

Item	Description
Dog	Puppy of mixed ancestry.
Piece of slipper	Much bitten. Unidentifiable.
Friend in room	Normally has slippers but no dog.
Residential home	10 residents, 3 staff, 1 dog.
Me	Just arrived. Puzzled.

Relationships—part

Dog is probably the one that lives here.
Dog has destroyed someone's slipper.
Slipper probably belonged to someone in the home, perhaps my friend but more likely one of the staff.
I am responsible for certain of my friend's needs, but not for the needs of others here.

Relationships—whole

The situation probably does not need my intervention, but I ought to make quite sure that my friend does not now need a new pair of slippers.

DIFFICULT PROBLEMS

Some situations are extremely complicated and therefore difficult to analyse. When trying to unravel the muddle of our thoughts we may sometimes become confused and feel like giving up before we have sorted things out properly. This is a perfectly natural reaction which we should expect to experience now and then, but which we should not give in to. As long as we have made a note of our findings as far as we have been able to go, we stand a good chance of being able to push the analysis further either through perseverance or by taking a break and returning to the task when we are rested.

If we have not sorted out the workings of the system satisfactorily we can regard the stumbling-block as a problem requiring attention. To identify and define this in terms of objective and obstacle will immediately open up new possibilities. Suppose, for example, that we are trying to make a diagram of the electrical wiring in a building and we come across a place where we are unable to follow each wire along. If we are able to define the problem as one in which the objective is to trace out the paths of certain wires, and the obstacle is that whereas three wires pass into the interior of a wall only two come out on the other side, then we have found something definite which we can concentrate upon and find a way of solving.

In a very simple example like this an intelligent person will have little difficulty in identifying, defining, and solving the problem, but if it is embedded in a complicated task he may not even notice that the problem is there, so he will not solve it and it will remain a permanent fault in his understanding of the whole system. This is a special kind of perceptual block—where the solver is unable to perceive the faults in his model or his interpretation of the system because of its complexity. There is one effective way of avoiding the risk of this kind of error. It is to explain our understanding of the system to another person and go on discussing it with him until he can see what we mean and finds it to be free from contradictions and inconsistencies. This person must be someone who is good at critical thinking. The challenge in having to explain a problem to someone else provides a useful discipline, which may bring forcibly to our attention some aspects of the problem where further understanding is needed. The other person whom we are enlisting to help us will be able to see flaws and gaps in our arguments better than we can, and will also feel a challenge to prove that our trust in his powers of thought is justified. We must then listen carefully to what he has to say and be prepared to follow up all his suggestions, even if what he says seems to be something we have already explored.

To benefit from other people's advice we have to be open-minded, because once we have come to a conclusion about how something works it is very hard to accept that somebody else's understanding of it is better than our own. Here is an example. A group of men who were devising a scheme for industrial training constructed a diagram of the system to help them in their thinking. What they were trying to explain to each other consisted of two separate but related systems, one was the annual cycle of planning and carrying out the training and the other was the long-term pattern of an individual person's career. However, they only drew one diagram in which these two different systems were confused. Strange to say, they were unable to see for themselves that anything was wrong with it. When the fault was pointed out to them they were still unable to see it and they insisted that their model was perfectly satisfactory. But I am sure it really must have been a considerable hindrance to them.

GROUP UNDERSTANDING

When interest in a problem is not confined to one person but is shared by a group, such as a family group, a social group, or a work group, obviously there is much to be said in favour of creating a common understanding of the problem amongst the members of the group. The problems belonging to a group need to be interpreted in the group.

The larger the group, the more need there is for control over discussion to make sure that all important issues are explored and that the members of the group advance together in their understanding. There is no better way to lead a discussion of this type than to use the method of analysis that we have been considering in this chapter, so as to provide an agenda of points that may require to be elucidated by the group. One way to do this is for the leader of the group to offer a definition of the problem and then to ask the group to derive from it a list of the elements of the problem. This can be written up on a board or a sheet of paper for all to see. The leader can then lead the discussion from item to item. When further discussion has taken place on the relations between the elements, a fairly consistent understanding of the problem will have been achieved by the group and the time will have been well spent. The way to test the results of this kind of discussion is simply to ask individual members to describe their interpretation in terms of the various component parts of the problem and of how one part relates to another.

A suitable method for controlling the later stages of discussion is to construct a model or diagram to represent what is being said and to relate each new contribution to it. An example from my own experience was the use of a means/ends block diagram. It was used to bring out the relationships between the objectives of various groups of people involved in a controversy over the use of artificial satellites in a communication system. This was useful in keeping the discussion to the point and holding the attention of the participants. It helped the whole group to keep together in discussion and to avoid breaking up into separate factions.

TESTS OF COMPLETION

Many of our problems are so deep and full of implications that there is no end to the amount of analysis to which we could subject them. But for practical purposes we must draw a line somewhere; we must be able to decide when the analysis has proceeded far enough and when we have understood enough, so we need to have a test that we can apply.

Fortunately there are one or two useful ways of testing whether or not we have gone far enough in this stage of problem-solving. As we have already indicated, if we can explain our interpretation of the problem situation to our own satisfaction and to the satisfaction of another person, and neither of us can see any ambiguities or contradictions or gaps in the explanation, we have evidently reached a reasonably thorough state of understanding. Alternatively, if we can draw a diagram or build a model which satisfactorily depicts all the essential features of the problem situation and their inter-relationships, that is also a convincing proof that we can interpret the problem satisfactorily.

Another test is to try to lay down a set of rules which describe completely how the system works, just as the rules of a game such as football are an interpretation of how the game works. This is a further example of the use of a word-model. If it is found that the set of rules is incomplete or inconsistent, then we have to look further in order to determine whether the fault lies in our interpretation of the rules or in the system itself.

The fact that we hope to be able to describe or to model our interpretation of the problem is something that we should bear in mind at the beginning of the interpretive stage. It is a target to aim at; something that can give us a clue to the sort of thinking and questioning processes we need to go through in our search for enlightenment.

SUMMARY

We have seen that the process of analysis can be described in four steps as follows:

1. Divide the situation or any available information about it into distinguishable parts.
2. Take each part or item by itself and study it until you know enough about it to be able to describe it.
3. State how the parts relate to each other and how they relate together to form the whole situation.
4. Study and describe critically the situation as a whole.

In other words, analysis takes a situation apart and puts it together again in a more understandable form. Analysis can be applied to any thing or situation, including passages of spoken and written language and technical and other systems. The objective and the obstacle or any given information about the problem may yield valuable insights if we analyse them. The analytical method when used in a group of people will help its members to come to a common understanding.

EXERCISES

1. Anthony Newley said, 'Stop the world, I want to get off!' What is your interpretation of this remark? Ask one or two other people for their interpretations also and compare results. Make sure that your interpretation is consistent with the emotional tone of the quotation.

2. Look through a newspaper and select the best example you can find of a piece of analytical writing. What do you think of it? How could it be improved?

3. Take a reader's letter published in a newspaper and analyse it. Re-write it as you would have expressed the ideas yourself.

4. Write down your own main objectives in life and also a list of your main activities in work and leisure. Do these fit well together?

5. Analyse what is going on where you are now.

6. Analyse your own thoughts at this moment.

7. What happens when someone reads a book?

8. What happens when two people have an argument?

9. What happens when someone attends a course of study?

10. Take a sentence in a foreign language with which you are not well acquainted and try to find out what each word means.

11. Here is a quotation from a report which seems to take two different attitudes towards competition between businesses, one that competition is good and the other that it is bad if it is unnecessary. Does this make sense?

> 'We saw competition as the main stimulus to efficiency but questioned, on the grounds of waste of resources, the validity of unnecessary competition, for example in the detergent and petrol fields.'

Is it reasonable to hold both views at the same time? Is the word 'competition' being used to refer to two different ideas? If so, what are they and what should they be called? Alternatively, do you think that the writer has accidentally expressed himself in a way which he did not intend and really meant to say that a moderate amount of competition is good but you can have too much of it? If so, what is meant by 'competition'? Define 'competition' in your own words and reconsider the statement after you have replaced 'competition' by your own definition.

Stage 3

CONSTRUCTING COURSES
OF ACTION

8

Strategies and Sources of Ideas

In previous chapters we have discussed the preparatory stages
of problem-solving and we come now to the creative and
constructive stage, in which one or more courses of action for
solving the problem are to be developed. As before, the best
preparation for it is to complete the previous stages thoroughly.
The best foundation is a clear definition of the problem and
a thorough understanding of all its important features and
their inter-relationships.

The work of constructing a course or courses of action has
to proceed from this starting point to a stage where one or
more feasible solutions have been worked out in sufficient
detail for it to be possible to move on to the next stage, which
is decision-making. We therefore need some ideas and we need
to select ones which will lead in the right direction. We need
to build them up and shape them so that they will come to
meet the requirements of our objective, so that the obstacle
that was originally in the way can be overcome and the
problem can be solved.

STRATEGIES

When we are faced with a new problem and there is sufficient
time available, we should consider it from both the strategic
and the tactical points of view. The strategic aspects, being
the broader considerations concerning the nature and direction

of the solution, should be looked at first, and they will provide a sound basis for working out the tactical details of how the objective is to be achieved.

There are four different types of strategy that we may apply:

> Strategies of timing
> Strategies of outcome
> Strategies of the objective
> Strategies of the obstacle.

STRATEGIES OF TIMING

Strategies of timing depend on the stage of development which the problem has reached by the time that we meet it, and on the rate at which it is becoming more urgent or the rate at which it is passing away. Here are three typical strategies in this class:

1. If we know enough about the problem we may be able to solve it while it still remains latent. For example, some diseases which can be detected and diagnosed by radiography can be cured before any noticeable symptoms ever arise.

2. If we notice the problem early we should try to solve it quickly, before it becomes more serious. For example, if pilfering is found to be taking place, the sooner it is stopped the less chance there will be that it will become serious.

3. If we leave the problem alone it may, in some circumstances, solve itself or come to nothing. For example, a man asked me to write a chapter for a book. I had insufficient time to do it because I was writing this book. Before long, he wrote and told me that the publishers had decided not to go ahead and that my chapter would not therefore be needed. In the example of a tree that has fallen across the road by the time we come to it the public authorities may have the matter in hand and someone may already be on the way to deal with it.

Strategies of Outcome

The way to tackle a problem depends upon the form of outcome that is required. If we are being asked to give advice about a decision that someone else has to make, such as whether or not to move a department of a business from one location to another, we could be required to make a simple statement of our opinion, or we could be required to produce an impressive report of many pages. If we know that the latter will be required, we are likely to embark on a much longer and more systematic investigation than we would for the former, where a relatively informal study would suit the informal outcome. Alternatively, we could be required to convince a third party of the truth and importance of our solution so that they would be eager to put it into effect. In such a case we might wish to involve the people concerned at the outset of the work of investigating the problem, so that they would be of the same mind as ourselves from the very beginning.

Strategies of the Objective

The fact that we know what our objective is does not imply that the only acceptable outcome is to achieve the objective completely. Nor does it imply that any other objective would be unacceptable as an alternative. On the contrary, we may have to be quite flexible in our approach if we are to achieve real success in the long run. Especially if the problem is a difficult one, a healthy attitude to adopt is to be prepared to consider a range of possible variations on what we are setting out to do. We could, in fact, regard our objective in a variety of different ways:

We could—go all out for it
—substitute another objective of similar value
—approximate to it
—modify it
—postpone it
—delegate it to someone else
—abandon it.

Strategies of the Obstacle

Likewise, it would be wrong to start off by regarding the obstacle as immutable. There are quite a number of different ways by which we might approach it. Here are some worth considering:

We might—overcome it
  —go round it
  —remove it
  —demolish it
  —neutralize it
  —prove it to be illusory
  —turn it to advantage (the most elegant of all strategies)
  —buy it off
  —alter it
  —find its weakest point
  —wait for it to go away.

To summarize briefly at this point, the first step in the constructive stage of problem-solving is to review the definition of the problem in the light of the interpretation that has been reached, and then decide upon the most appropriate timing of action. Next, determine what form of outcome is wanted, from which the amount and nature of the work to be done in solving the problem can be estimated. At the same time it is important to think about the approach to be taken to the objective and to the obstacle, whether to go all out for the objective by way of an overwhelming assault on the obstacle or use a more restrained or subtle form of attack.

After setting the broad strategic lines of approach to the problem we come to one of the most interesting and satisfying phases, where we have to collect the ideas needed to produce a solution. We must be prepared to work hard to get the right ideas because the quality and success of the outcome depend upon them. Sometimes it is wise to delay the attack on a problem because the ideas do not readily come to mind, but when time is not on our side we may need to search actively for the ideas we want.

As in any other searching situation we can manage the search for ideas better if we plan it systematically, first making sure what we are looking for, determining which are the most likely places where it might be found, and then choosing suitable methods of searching.

By now it should be perfectly clear what kind of ideas we are looking for because the whole purpose of considering the timing, outcome, objective, and obstacle strategically is to bring into focus the issues which really matter.

Next comes the question of where to look for ideas. On any occasion the following sources of ideas may be useful.

SOURCES OF IDEAS

1. Ourselves.
2. Other people.
   (*a*) Those concerned in the problem.
   (*b*) Other people with 'a fresh mind'.
   (*c*) Experts.
3. Books and other writings.

OURSELVES AS SOURCES OF IDEAS

We naturally look to our own personal resources first when we have any kind of problem and it is particularly wise to do so when we are seeking ideas. Our own ideas can come directly from current experience of events in which we are involved or of which we are spectators, or from memories of past experience. We shall begin our study of this topic by considering some aspects of the process of creative thinking. Next we shall look for ways of making better use of our experiences, and then we shall review the environmental conditions which affect the efficiency of creative thought. A considerable number of techniques and methods which anyone can use in the generation of ideas will be described in the next chapter, following a review of the other main sources from which ideas can be obtained.

THE CREATIVE THOUGHT PROCESS

The process by which creative thought is produced has been a subject of interest to philosophers and psychologists throughout the ages. One of the earliest discoveries in this field was the theory of association of ideas, as propounded by Aristotle and others. In the early 1920s G. Spearman, one of the pioneers in the development of intelligence tests, put forward his theory of 'noegenesis', which explains how new ideas are created in the mind. He distinguished three ways in which this happens. The first is 'the apprehension of experience', which means that we derive ideas from immediate experience and also by being aware of ourselves as receivers of experience. The second is 'the eduction of relations', which means that we discover the relations between ideas. This is similar to the theory of association. The third is 'the eduction of correlates', which means that when we have in mind both an idea and a relation, we can think of a second idea which is connected to the first idea by the given relation. More developments in the theory of thought processes have taken place recently, but many of these early theories have not yet out-lived their usefulness.

The stages through which creative thinking passes are another popular theme in the literature of this subject. Graham Wallas, in his book *The Art of Thought*, published in 1926, listed four stages as follows:

> Preparation
> Incubation
> Illumination
> Verification.

'Preparation' means studying the problem thoroughly, as we have discussed in the first two stages of the system of problem-solving followed in this book. 'Incubation' means that a period of time is required for the mind to digest and recombine the information that has been gathered. 'Illumination' is the event which occurs when the happy thought for solving the problem arrives in consciousness. Illumination was described by Wallas as sometimes being associated with a special feeling of 'intimation', which means a feeling of heightened consciousness occurring at the moment of insight. 'Verification' is self-explanatory but does not always seem to occur in practice and therefore, although desirable, is presumably not an essential part of the creative process.

Apart from drawing attention to the importance of preparation and incubation, to know how to describe the stages of creative thinking in this manner is not by itself much help towards learning how to think more effectively, but at least it shows us what to expect to happen when we have to consider some difficult matter creatively.

INTUITIVE THINKING

There is an obvious contrast between the kind of thinking described by Wallas and intuitive thinking. Intuitive thought, given that it is immediate and not dependent upon reason, is potentially vastly more economical than thought which involves study and reflection. Unfortunately, it would not be a sound policy to do all our thinking by intuition in order to save the time and effort required for normal reasoned thought. We cannot guarantee to produce an intuitive idea whenever we need one, and in any case, there is a good chance that an intuitive idea will turn out to be wrong.

Nevertheless, there are times when our only chance of success depends upon making an instant decision. We should learn to distinguish such occasions from the normal situation, so that when it is right to take short cuts in thinking we should feel confidently justified in doing so and put forward our ideas without hesitation. Also, there is no harm in trying to think quickly as long as we take enough care over the verification stage, and in any case, the ability to think more rapidly improves naturally as a result of practising a methodical approach to problem-solving.

Perhaps the best way to regard intuitive ideas is to give them serious consideration when they occur to us spontaneously, because a successful hunch may produce big returns from a small outlay; but not to try to cultivate a deliberately intuitive approach to serious problems because of the high level of risk that this would entail.

OPPORTUNISM

Opportunism is the art of adapting policy to circumstances. In problem-solving generally it is always useful, but in constructing courses of action it is especially valuable. It depends on several component skills which we should try to cultivate. Firstly, it depends upon the ability to retain a broad outlook at all times, even when concentrating on a specific problem. Only by keeping an eye on the state of affairs outside the immediate problem-situation is it possible to notice what resources can be brought in to help solve the problem. In business, for example, some managers make sure that they are aware of new techniques of management so that they can apply them when occasions arise, whereas others struggle away at their problems in ignorance of the fact that simple routine methods for solving them have already been worked out. Some motorists know many routes for their journeys to work, but a person who knows only one route will not know how to get past a traffic hold-up when one develops on his way.

Secondly, as Louis Pasteur said, 'Change arises from the impact of a new idea on a prepared mind.' We only act on an opportunity if we are ready for it, which means that it is a good investment to spend time in thinking about new ventures well in advance.

Thirdly, opportunism depends on the desire to store up things and ideas which are not particularly useful at the time they are discovered, but are seen to have potential for application at some future date. Some people like to collect materials, tools, books, or ideas that look interesting, just because they 'might come in useful some day'. They keep pieces of timber to think about in the garage, or pieces of irreplaceable mechanism in the loft. Such people are advised not to consort with the kind of person who likes to be extremely neat and tidy, because their attitudes to life are not easy to reconcile, but the collector is likely to be well equipped for opportunism, as long as he can remember what he has in store and where he put it!

Fourthly, opportunism depends on the possession of means of storage and retrieval. The ability to store real things depends upon the possession of accommodation and storage equipment, which is costly, but ideas can be stored without much complication or cost. It is useful and inexpensive to carry a pocket-notebook for recording ideas when they are first thought of, and to keep some sort of filing system at home or in the office for the storage and classification of notes and references. The only proviso is to keep one's records under regular review, because once they have been forgotten they will remain forgotten and will never be put to practical use.

SERENDIPITY

In 1754 Horace Walpole coined this word, which is derived from a fairy-tale about the 'Three Princes of Serendip', who 'were always making discoveries, by accident and sagacity, of things they were not in quest of'. Serendip is an old name for the island of Ceylon, and 'serendipity' means the art of making happy discoveries by chance. Presumably, it is related in some way to inquisitiveness and curiosity, but essentially the possession of serendipity is a matter of good fortune rather than a skill that we can cultivate deliberately. Nevertheless it is an entirely charming idea, and if we are acquainted with its meaning and believe in it perhaps we may be inspired with some of its magical quality and become luckier in our experience of opportunities of all kinds.

Apparently, some of the brilliant ideas that contributed to the success of the famous Ealing Comedy Films came about through a combination of opportunism and serendipity. The main idea on which the film 'Passport to Pimlico' was based was a real event which occurred in Canada, where a group of local people tried to set themselves up as a separate little country. A newspaper-cutting describing this incident lay in the possession of the author of the film story for a long time before he rediscovered it and realized that here was the germ of an unusual and entertaining plot. The idea of smuggling gold in the shape of a souvenir of the Eiffel Tower, which was used in the film 'The Lavender Hill Mob', was derived from an actual souvenir of this type which happened to be lying about in someone's desk.

Many scientific discoveries came about through people

saving up promising ideas until their true value had become apparent. In 1883 Thomas Edison carried out some experiments to try to prevent the blackening of the envelope of electric lamps which was caused by a deposit of carbon thrown off from the filament. He put a metal plate between the filament and the glass and discovered that if he connected the plate to the positive terminal of the supply a small current passed in the plate circuit, and he also observed that when the plate was connected to the negative terminal no current flowed.

J. Ambrose Fleming, who was the Professor of Electrical Engineering at University College, London, repeated his experiments and made the further discovery that when he fed the lamp from an alternating current supply a direct current could be drawn from the plate. This work was described in a paper given to the Royal Society in 1890. Fleming kept the apparatus used in these experiments whilst he got on with other work, and then in 1904 completed the development of a practical thermionic valve using one of the same devices as in the earlier experiments. This is a clear example of an inventor not realizing the potential value of his discoveries but succeeding eventually because he did not throw away his old equipment and his old ideas.

Sometimes when an experiment goes wrong it gives the scientist an entirely new phenomenon to think about. This was the case in the discovery of analine dyes when an attempt to synthesize quinine failed, and also in the discovery of hormone weedkillers when an attempt to use hormones for stimulating plant growth proved to be too drastic.

PERSEVERANCE AND METHOD

It is apparent to anyone who reads detective stories that if the crime is not solved by a stroke of luck or genius it is solved by the application of perseverance and method. The latter are equally applicable to problems outside the world of crime fiction and we may well consider how to develop them, bearing in mind that in real life even geniuses depend upon both perseverance and method to bring their projects to completion.

To persevere with a difficult problem is a practical way of extending our capabilities beyond what we can accomplish in a more limited assault. It is natural and sensible to recoil after an initial uusuccessful attempt, especially to reconsider our tactics and to re-muster our resources, but what is most important is to return to the attack and keep on returning until we have succeeded in doing what we set out to do. 'If at first you don't succeed, try, try again.' On the other hand, perseverance may not be sufficient if the method is inadequate. To give a simple example, I saw an old lady playing a game of patience. She had the cards laid out in ten columns and at each turn of play she was looking for opportunities to make advantageous moves. But she was tired and the complexity of the game was almost too much for her. It was clear that she was playing unsystematically and her attention returned again and again to the situation right in the middle of the field of view, like a moth being drawn to a lamp. The cards at the extreme left and extreme right of the game might just as well have not been there at all. If only she could have adopted a methodical procedure of starting at the left and examining each pile of cards in turn to determine whether or not a move was possible, she would have been able to make much better progress and obtain much more satisfaction from playing the game. Playing patience may seem trivial to many of us, although it is not so trivial if it is one of the few pastimes within one's physical capacity. But the value of this example is its analogy with other kinds of problem. If we have a sound method and we persevere with it, we can make sure that a whole range of possibilities are fully and efficiently explored.

A classical example of the methodical approach pursued relentlessly was the discovery of radium by the Curies. They were looking for radio-active substances, and they knew how to test for the properties they were seeking. They obtained very large numbers of mineral substances and applied their tests systematically and painstakingly to every one, working on and on for years until they discovered at last what they were looking for. Here was a situation where no amount of intuition could enable a short cut to be made. They just had to persevere until they reached the goal.

The methodical and the intuitive ways of making a discovery are not incompatible because they can occur together, either when a creative leap is made in the course of a thoroughly methodical investigation, or when a methodical search has proved that the solution cannot lie in a certain direction and therefore a new line of enquiry must be found.

The capacity to persevere is also worth developing for the sake of its long-term benefits. By persevering in any activity we develop our skills.

CONDITIONS REQUIRED FOR CREATIVE THOUGHT

In Chapter 5 we gave some attention to the conditions required for interpretive thought. Creative thought is not quite the same as interpretive thought and sometimes is best done in slightly different circumstances. But it is still a very personal matter. We should find out what conditions are most favourable for us individually and make sure that they are present when it is important to do our best creative work.

Some people are self-stimulating when it comes to producing ideas, and others rely more upon inspiration or encouragement from their fellows. Some get their best ideas in the warm and luxurious atmosphere of the bathroom; others prefer a cool or even a spartan environment. Some prefer to be relaxed; others to be under the pressure of working to a deadline. If we know what conditions suit us best, that is excellent. If we do not, we can easily try different sorts of environment and see how they work out. It is as well, however, to take care not to assume too readily that our feelings are a true indication of what is really good or bad for us. It has been demonstrated by experiment that noise, for example, does not always have a bad effect on performance, even when it is distinctly annoying.

The more usual state of affairs, especially when we are trying to be creative at our place of employment, is that we remain too passive and do not make the necessary effort to obtain the right kind of conditions at the appropriate time. People who work in noisy factories, for example, do not make the effort to get away to a place of quiet when they need to think about a difficult work problem. Usually in such cases it is nothing more than the force of tradition which prevents them from moving to a quieter place such as a library, park, training centre, or even their own home to do some creative thinking.

GETTING IDEAS FROM OTHER PEOPLE

It is all very well to be self-reliant and self-sufficient, but the fact is that there may well be other people around who know more about the problem than we do ourselves and are already in possession of appropriate ideas for its solution. There may be others who can understand the problem better than us because they have a fresh mind or are more inquisitive, intelligent, or imaginative. To some managers attending courses on problem-solving it comes as a powerful shock to discover that other people can help them with their problems, having been convinced that they were the only people who knew enough about their field of work to be able to understand it properly.

THOSE CONCERNED IN THE PROBLEM

During my experience of investigating industrial problems it has often been evident that plenty of good ideas for solving them are available on the spot. The people who actually do the work in the area where the problem has been identified usually know a great deal about what could be done to improve the system. The task of the investigator in these circumstances is to gather the ideas, evaluate them, and communicate the best of them to the management. This observation, which is by no means unique, implies that many problems could be solved more quickly and to everyone's greater satisfaction if communications in industry were better. Strangely, some people refuse to accept responsibility for collecting ideas from their subordinates and they expect outside consultants to do it for them. No wonder they have problems!

An acquaintance once asked me for advice about how to deal with his son's wild and disturbing behaviour. The father had never actually asked his son to say why he behaved as he did. I advised him that it was time to do so and gave some suggestions as to how to put the question. It turned out that the son was quite willing and able to explain the cause of his behaviour to his father. The cause was an event which had occurred many years before and he was able to suggest what was needed to make things better. From that moment the personal relations between father and son took a new direction and began to improve steadily, all as a result of asking the person really concerned to give his own views about the problem.

There is usually a price to be paid, however. When we go to someone for advice we must be prepared to listen sympathetically to whatever he has to say. We cannot expect him to give out the 'pure gold' without a fair amount of less valuable material as well. Most people do not have enough opportunity to talk about matters that are important to them with somebody who takes an interest. So when somebody comes to them for advice their main desire is to express themselves by telling the enquirer about their troubles and their pet ideas. It is only fair to accept this treatment graciously as a way of meeting the other person's needs. To do so is an essential process in building up bonds of trust between ourselves and our fellows.

Those who are closest to the nub of the problem may also run the greatest risk of being biased in their outlook. For this reason it is dangerous to accept suggestions uncritically. Ideas offered to us should be checked out logically in relation to our own interpretation of the problem to see whether they make sense or not. If they look promising, they should be balanced against the views of other people concerned in the situation before we make up our minds whether or not to incorporate them in our solution.

OTHER PEOPLE WITH A FRESH MIND

Perhaps the most difficult art in collecting ideas from other people is to get someone who is not already involved in a problem to suggest ideas which we can accept. People who wish to agree with our own ideas or congratulate us on our ingenuity are very rare creatures. Other people usually want to be original as much as we ourselves do, and they may find it more interesting to disagree with us than to agree. They are also most unlikely to see the problem the way we do because their experience has been different.

I find that it is necessary to be very selective about this and have certain people to whom I can go for advice about one sort of problem and others for advice about other sorts of problems, leaving a residue of certain people to whom it is fatal to go for advice on anything.

Other people can help properly only if they are given a clear explanation of what the problem is all about. This is a two-way process which is bound to take time and requires on our part patience and sensitive attention to their reactions. Then we must be able to listen attentively and be prepared to open our minds to ideas which may be in conflict with our own. The other person will respond if we make approving comments about his suggestions and ask questions which give further challenge to his intellect. Above all, the greatest essential is to come clean. People cannot and will not give us their full co-operation unless we reveal the whole of the problem to them. It is no use telling them only a part of the story or asking them hypothetical questions. They will only be able to think in the way we want them to think if we put them fully in the picture. This is just as true of accidental omission of information as of deliberate concealment. It is all too easy in our enthusiasm to assume that our willing collaborator knows as much as we do about the problem and to forget that he has only just heard of it. And since it is boring to be told what one already knows, it is tactful to ask whether we are giving him too much or too little information when we explain the background and circumstances of the problem.

EXPERTS

It may require a little courage and tact to get help from a world-class expert, but even this is possible. A friend of mine wanted to get some advice on the subject of motivating people at work. He found out that there was shortly to be a conference on the subject in New York at which the world's experts would be present. He decided to take this opportunity to meet the men who were really going to be able to give him the advice he needed. So he sent off for a reservation for the conference and bought an airline ticket to go there all the way from London. He then went to the conference and made sure that he met the men he wanted to see personally so that he could put his questions directly to them.

From my own experience I know that many experts will respond to a politely worded letter requesting advice and it seems that the more eminent a person is the more likely he is to reply.

I have an acquaintance whose job it is to collect ideas from experts and pass them on to people in industry to help them to solve their problems. But experts can be just as loquacious as anybody else. His advice about how to get them to give their advice briefly and to stick to the point is to conduct as much business as possible by telephone. This puts the person at the other end in a situation in which he is used to compressing his message into as few words as possible.

BOOKS AND OTHER WRITINGS

Most of the problems we face have occurred in a similar form to other people. Not just one or two people, but thousands and millions. Among that multitude there are sure to have been dedicated thinkers who had some success in solving these problems and took the trouble to record their findings in books and other forms of the printed word for the benefit of others.

It is really amazing to contemplate the enormous range of subjects that have been covered in this way. People who take an interest in books are well aware of it, but there are many others who are not familiar with the world of books at all. A visit to a large bookshop or the non-fiction section of a public library will give some impression of the range of subjects on which useful books have been written, but it is really necessary to see the lists of books issued by specialist publishers or to go to a large central library to appreciate fully what is available.

Whatever subject interests us, whether we are stamp

collectors or debt collectors, whether we want to make profits or make friends and influence people, there is a book which can help. The only difficult part is to remember this fact at the right time. To lay hands on the right book is usually easy because people in libraries and bookshops are knowledgeable and are generally very willing to give advice and assistance.

The best policy is to build up a collection of books to cover the sorts of problem that we most commonly have to solve and draw upon the services of local libraries or a library at work, if there is one, for the unusual. I suppose the most useful of all books is a dictionary, because there are so many problems in the use of words, and therefore everyone ought to have access to a dictionary both at home and at work. After that an encyclopaedia is the next most useful kind of book to keep because it can provide some sort of an answer to a large number of possible questions and give many a clue to the whereabouts of further information that we are seeking.

For all the availability of books on so many subjects it is surprising how little some people respect them. When we need information on some special point we are inclined either to procrastinate or to go and ask someone else rather than to make a point of looking it up. Once I was visited by an investigator working for a government department, who brought a list of questions to ask about my work. One of the questions he asked was about the sources of ideas I used in a particular and important part of my work. He suggested several possible sources, such as courses of training on that particular subject, consultants, other companies, and the Industry Training Board. None of these was the true answer. The answer was that I had based my work on information obtained from books, which were able to cover the subject more thoroughly and clearly than any of the sources the investigator had expected me to use.

Other media such as films, sound recordings on disc and tape, and computers are coming into use for the storage and communication of recorded ideas. Although they are not yet as widely available as books they offer new and valuable ways of interacting with a source of information and are likely to have a great influence on the pattern of our lives in the future.

The literature of problem-solving and other related matters

is itself large and extremely interesting. There is a section at the end of this book which contains details of several books which should be useful to anyone who may wish to study the subject further and in greater detail.

SUMMARY

The methodological approach to problem-solving makes sure that we find out as soon as possible what really matters in each problem we tackle. When we understand our objectives, the obstacles to them, the importance of timing and the type of outcome that we are aiming to produce, we are able to think strategically. When we have chosen a strategy we are in a better position to know what kinds of ideas we need to accomplish our purpose.

Ideas can come from ourselves, other people, or books and other media of recorded information. The collection of ideas is a creative process which is affected by the conditions in which we work and by the methods we use.

EXERCISES

1. Classify the following situations according to the type of strategies which could be applied to them, i.e. strategies of timing, strategies of outcome, strategies of the objective, strategies of the obstacle.

    (a) You are an expert on the subject of transport and have been invited to give a talk about it in three months' time.

    (b) You are a manufacturer. One of your products has never really been satisfactory and is still giving trouble.

    (c) You intend to build a new rose-bed in your garden next year, but the nurseryman from whom you prefer to buy roses is going to close down his business before then.

    (d) You are wrapping up a parcel to send by post and find that it weighs just enough to put the cost of postage up by a considerable amount.

2. What alternative strategies might be available in each of

the examples above? For instance, the expert on transport could prepare his talk in different ways to suit different kinds of audience, or he might prepare the talk now or leave it until nearer the time.

3. Opportunities lie all around us, waiting to be recognized. Make a list of three or four problems that concern you currently. Now look around the room or wherever you are at this moment and choose five or six things that you can see. Consider each of these in turn and ask yourself what idea it suggests that could help to solve one or other of your problems. For example a telephone might suggest better communications, or a book might suggest further study of the subject.

4. Think of one of your own problems which you are finding difficult to persevere with, such as trying to finish a tedious job. Divide the work into small portions which can be completed in a reasonable amount of time and write in your diary when you will do them. Structured work is usually easier to do than unstructured work so this should help you to achieve a little success, which in turn will enable you to regard perseverance itself as a more pleasant and rewarding kind of behaviour.

5. What circumstances affect you most when you are trying to think creatively? Are the conditions in which you are best able to think creatively the same as those in which you are best able to think analytically? If not, what are the differences?

6. It is essential to raise £2,000 for repairs to the premises of a sports club. The objective is to get the club house repaired and the obstacle is a lack of money. What strategies should be considered for attacking this problem? What gaps in our knowledge of the situation need to be filled?

7. A sack of potatoes has to be carried by hand for 50 metres, but there is a hole in it big enough for potatoes to fall through. What strategies would you consider? What courses of action would follow from them?

8. Assuming that you have a garden, how would you go about designing a garden shed to put in it? Where would you get suitable ideas from?

9. Go to the library and enquire about books on problem-solving or any other subject which may interest you.
10. Ask someone for advice and consider afterwards whether you used the encounter to the best advantage.
11. Why is it important to find out the objectives of other people concerned in the problems we are trying to solve?
12. If you had the task of writing a book on your favourite subject, how would you start to collect ideas for it? How would you divide the material up into chapters?
13. How could a person who was born deaf be helped to understand something of the enjoyment of listening to or making music?
14. Why is it difficult to help poor people to improve their standard of living?

9

Techniques for Generating Ideas

From the literature on the subject of how to create new ideas and from personal sources we shall be considering twenty or so different idea-generating techniques. They can be classified for convenience into four distinct groups, representative of the following four basic methods by which the creation of new ideas can be assisted.

1. Freeing the mind from inhibiting influences.
2. Utilizing past experience.
3. Artificially bringing different ideas into conjunction.
4. Exploiting the mind's natural tendency to explore the unknown and to complete ideas that are incomplete.

I have not attempted to include all known methods in this collection. Some readers with special knowledge of the subject may wonder why their favourite methods of generating ideas are not mentioned. In some instances it is merely a matter of ignorance on my part, but I have deliberately excluded some methods which I regard as advanced or sophisticated and suitable more for people who are employed exclusively in creative work than for the general reader.

FREEING THE MIND FROM INHIBITING INFLUENCES

Our mental apparatus has facilities for producing ideas in great variety, but it also possesses means for sifting out ideas which are inappropriate on a given occasion and for generally keeping our thought processes under control. These means can be likened to a system of censorship or a braking system. They serve important purposes by preventing us from saying or doing the wrong thing and from mental over-activity. Without them our behaviour would be chaotic. Nevertheless, it is possible to use simple and harmless methods to relax the censorship or take off the brakes in order to give the imagination greater freedom and permit a greater flow of ideas.

More Blocks

The emotional, perceptual, and cultural blocks which we considered in Chapter 5 in relation to the stage of interpretation are relevant again at this point, as blocks to creative thought. Two varieties of perceptual block which especially affect the ability to produce new ideas are vested interests and the recency of similar experience.

Vested interests prevent us from thinking effectively about possible courses of action which run contrary to our own biased personal interests. An example of this might be that we are 'empire-builders', and cannot bring ourselves to contemplate any solution to a problem which would cause someone else's 'empire' to grow rather than our own.

Recency of similar experience causes us to assume that if the problem we are at present tackling is at all similar to one that we have recently solved successfully, we are likely to want to apply the same solution even though, in truth, there may be differences in the situation which make such an assumption invalid.

Here are two examples. Children at school who have just learnt a method of solving a certain type of mathematical problem often try to apply it to whatever type of problem they next meet, whether it is suitable or not. When our telephone at home rings at a particular time of day we may jump to the conclusion that it is a call for the same person who received a call at that time on another recent occasion.

The way we can learn to avoid blocks to creativity is to find out which kinds of block we are susceptible to. This we can most readily do by looking back over our thought processes whenever we find that we have not solved a problem as efficiently as we would have liked. Having identified blocks to which we are prone, we can prepare ourselves to avoid or reject them the next time we have to deal with a similar problem, and thus begin to develop better habits of thought.

AVOIDANCE OF CRITICISM

One of the most powerful of influences is the psychological atmosphere in which we work. It is very difficult to produce new ideas in a situation where the predominant attitude is one of criticism. For this reason, people who are in charge of creative workers should always try to avoid taking up a critical attitude, and should try to prevent critical attitudes from developing among their staff. The same principle applies when we are working on our own. If we want to produce new ideas freely we should not subject our suggestions to criticism, but let them come out just as they are. To do this we need to be able to defer judgement; the time to judge the value of our ideas is not when they are newly emerging from their source, but at a later stage when they have been expressed more fully and we have had a chance to get used to them.

EMPHASIS ON QUANTITY

Usually we are very careful in trying to solve a problem. We only need one solution, so we explore one possibility at a time, developing the idea gradually and persistently until it can be seen whether it will work or not. An opposite approach which can sometimes be just as effective is to throw caution to the winds and go all out for producing as many ideas as possible that might have some bearing on the solution.

If we place the emphasis on quantity, as opposed to quality, we are less likely to be inhibited in our thinking and are more likely to be able to produce original ideas.

CREATIVE MOMENTUM

Once the ideas begin to flow, a certain kind of creative momentum develops which helps to prevent our critical

faculties from coming into operation and producing an in-
hibitory effect. This is sometimes called 'free-wheeling'. To
keep the momentum up we must be prepared to put forward
ideas which normally we would regard as unrealistic or even
ridiculous. This principle is closely related to the avoidance
of criticism and the suspension of judgement, both of which
can have a powerful influence on the momentum of the flow
of ideas.

Fluency Exercises

It is fact that most people can be helped to increase their
fluency in producing ideas by means of practice under favourable conditions. A leader can give a group of people suitable
exercises to do, or we can practise on our own, once we know
how to do it. Most of the effect of this practice wears off after
a little while, but it can be re-generated quickly on another
occasion. In some people, however, practice can produce a
permanent improvement in creative fluency, especially if the
exercises are tailor-made to overcome their own particular
difficulties.

A typical fluency exercise is carried out by taking any
simple object like a pencil or a handkerchief and trying to
write down as many different possible uses of it as we can
think of in one minute. Most people who have not done this
sort of thing before manage to think of about five different
uses of the object, some only one or two and some as many
as ten. With practice many people can produce about ten
suggestions in a minute. Those who find it hard to produce
ideas tend to think only of the obvious; they can only think
about what they have actually experienced. For them a pencil
is to write with, or to make holes in a piece of paper. Those
who are more fluent in their creative thinking can produce a
proportion of more unexpected and strange ideas. For them
a pencil can be to conduct an orchestra with or to make bars
for a cage for a small animal, and so on.

When a group of people are working together to solve a
problem and come to a stage where they really have to search
hard for new ideas, this type of exercise can be very helpful in
'warming them up' for their task, particularly if it is made

clear to them that it is the quantity of ideas that matters at this stage rather than the quality.

A few years ago this approach was used to help someone I know to overcome a difficulty in writing compositions for school work. He had a lively imagination but was unable to write his ideas down freely. On two or three occasions he was given some exercises designed to separate the thinking part of the process of composition from the writing part. The writing was done for him at first, until he had learned that he really did have the ability to produce interesting and useful ideas. Then he was given practice in composing a given set of ideas into a story and then later all the skills of creating ideas, composition, and writing were practised together. Without much fuss or difficulty he became reasonably good at writing compositions and it is evident that he has retained this facility to the present time.

BRAINSTORMING

Brainstorming is a popular and interesting procedure for gathering ideas. It was developed by Alex Osborn by bringing together a number of different idea-generating techniques. It is effective and has the advantage of helping people to work together, although it has limitations, as we shall see later. The technique has several variations of form, but in order to avoid confusion we shall consider only one version here.

The leader of a brainstorming session should begin by choosing the group of people who are to take part. Frequently the group is brought together specifically for the brainstorming session, but any group such as a committee can be turned into a brainstorming group if it wishes, as long as the leader knows what to do. The size of the group is not of great importance, but it is best to have between ten and twenty people. The members should be those who will co-operate well in trying to produce new ideas and should not include people who are likely to be domineering or critical or silent.

The leader should make preparations by choosing a reasonably comfortable room of appropriate size for the group, and by providing sufficient blackboards or large writing surfaces on which to write the hundred or so ideas that may be generated during the proceedings.

When the group has assembled, and if the members have not 'brainstormed' before, the leader should explain that the purpose of the session is to produce as many ideas as possible relating to the subject in hand. He will then tell the group about the four rules of brainstorming, which are as follows:

> Suspend judgement
> Quantity
> Free-wheeling
> Cross-fertilize.

Suspend judgement is the advice we have already referred to as 'defer judgement' under the heading of 'Avoidance of criticism'. Quantity and free-wheeling are also topics that we have discussed under the general heading of 'Freeing the mind from inhibiting influences'. The fourth rule of cross-fertilization, however, is of a different type. It is one of the methods of 'artificially bringing different ideas into conjunction' in order to produce further ideas, a class of method that we shall be coming to shortly. The rule of cross-fertilization means that we should try to build on other ideas, those of other people as well as our own. The four rules should be explained to the group and displayed prominently so that everybody can be reminded of them in the course of the session.

The next step is to give two or three warming-up fluency exercises to the group so as to get the ideas flowing and to accustom the members to working together informally in creative work.

The attention of the group should then be brought to the problem in hand. This is done by expressing the problem in the 'how to . . .' form described in Chapter 4 as 'definition for method'. Four or five different versions of the statement of the problem should be written up on the blackboard so as to cause the group to start thinking about a wide range of relevant aspects of the problem.

Example

Let us suppose that we are the committee of a club devoted to the pursuit of some sort of recreational activity. The club needs more members and we are having a brainstorming session to try to get some ideas for solving the problem. The leader of the session may suggest a formulation of the problem in these terms: 'How to increase membership'. This will be written up for all to see. Alternative versions of the problem will then be added, such as: 'How to increase the numbers of young members', 'How to increase public interest in the club', or 'How to promote the growth of the club'.

It is usual for the list of versions of the problem to contain some statements which are narrower in their meaning than the original formulation and others which are broader. When five or six have been listed, those present will choose the one which covers the situation best and looks most likely to inspire useful ideas. This will be re-expressed in the form of a question inviting a quantity of suggestions, such as 'In how many ways can we help to promote the growth of the club?' and left on display throughout the session.

The leader will then ask the members of the group for their ideas and will write up an abbreviated version of each suggestion for all to see. He will repeat each item as he writes, and will number each one so that it can be easily identified in sequence. He will accept all suggestions without comment or criticism, and will only intervene to ask for explanations of obscure items or to encourage members to follow the rules.

When twenty minutes or so have passed the session will be stopped, and it will be decided what to do with the results. One useful way to deal with them is to classify them into groups of similar ideas and choose one or two of the best from each group to put to practical use. This work should be done on a separate occasion from the brainstorming session itself. Before leaving the collection of ideas a further way of putting them to work is to take one or two of the 'wildest' ideas and 'twist' them or otherwise modify them so that they are turned from something unlikely to be of any use into something of real practical value.

A topic for brainstorming does not have to be light-hearted in character, for the method can be applied effectively to serious and even sombre problems. I took part recently in a brainstorming session which tackled the problem of finding ways to sustain the morale of a group of workers of whom one was suffering from an incurable disease. The session produced many useful and acceptable ideas without once becoming either morbid or insensitive.

A useful method for extracting ideas of a more general nature from the results of a brainstorming session is as follows. Take the first idea on the list and try to think of a useful principle which it illustrates. This will probably come out as a very rough or vague concept. Then look at all the other ideas in turn to see which of them are similar to the first and can be used to refine the emerging principle. In this manner more and more examples are examined until the principle which underlies them becomes clear enough to be accepted as a permanent guide. The ideas which have been found to relate to the first idea can then be crossed off the list and the process can then be repeated.

When working with my colleague Tim Pearce, who gave this method the name 'The Computer Sort', we were considering a list of ideas he had collected on the subject of how to manage the use of time. The first idea we looked at was 'adequate lighting'. This suggested something to do with physical comfort or conditions of work. Then we looked at 'legible writing', 'don't look at view outside', 'put mental notes on paper', and some others, and soon came to the conclusion that these were all examples of the efficient use of the human senses. From this we derived the guiding principle that one way to manage the use of time is 'to know the strengths and weaknesses of our physical senses and use them efficiently', so that we can be sure that the time that is available is not wasted through inefficient use of our senses.

Much research has been done on the effectiveness of the brainstorming technique. It has been found that the quality of ideas produced by group brainstorming is in fact no greater than that which can be produced by an equal number of people 'brainstorming' separately, so there is no absolute advantage in using this method in groups. However, it is much easier to manage the situation in a group because it can be set up more quickly than with an equal number of separate people, and it helps in developing a team spirit and in gaining acceptance of new proposals.

UTILIZING PAST EXPERIENCE

Another aspect of the mind capable of exploitation is that it is a storehouse of useful information. In it there are traces of our whole lifetime of experience, among which are quantities of ideas relevant to today's problems. What we need is a repertoire of methods for retrieving useful information from the store.

I have only three items to offer under this heading, so perhaps this is a field where further developments in method could be made. I have deliberately left out a discussion of the many established methods for so-called memory training, because they are well described in other books and in any case seem to be more suitable to help in the memorization of facts than the recall of past experience.

QUESTIONING TECHNIQUES

This extract from a little poem by Rudyard Kipling shows that he was well aware of the value of asking questions to gain access to stored human experience.

> 'I keep six honest serving men,
> They taught me all I knew
> Their names are What and Why and When
> And How and Where and Who.'

It is easy to make up special questions to elicit the information we need, and we can use lists of questions which have been built up by specialists and are available in various books, such as A. L. Simberg's *Creativity at Work* and Alex Osborn's *Applied Imagination*.

It was recognized several decades ago by the exponents of work simplification that questions may be asked for two special purposes. One kind of question is for fact finding; it sets out to elicit factual information. The other is challenging;

it asks for specific contributions to the solution of the problem. These two types of question can be delivered in combination, like a one-two punch. We first ask the fact-finding question and then we follow up with a series of challenging questions which either probe into the reasons behind the facts or demand alternatives. Here is a typical set of work simplification questions.

PURPOSE — WHAT are we trying to do?
WHY is it done?
What ELSE could be done?
What SHOULD be done?

PLACE — WHERE is it done?
WHY is it done THERE?
Where ELSE could it be done?
Where SHOULD it be done?

SEQUENCE — WHEN is it done?
WHY is it done THEN?
When ELSE could it be done?
When SHOULD it be done?

PERSON — WHO does it?
WHY does THAT person do it?
Who ELSE could do it?
Who SHOULD do it?

MEANS — How is it done?
WHY is it done THAT WAY?
How ELSE could it be done?
How SHOULD it be done?

Questioning is one of the few creative techniques which should not be recommended without qualification. The reason for this is that it is regarded by some people as restrictive to the imagination. If this is true, the method of questioning is not particularly suitable for the first attack on a problem, but should be kept in reserve for use when other methods have been exhausted.

CRITICAL INCIDENTS

In 1933 the National Institute of Industrial Psychology was helping Imperial Airways to improve their method of selecting young men to take charge of the business side of its air stations abroad. Alec Rodger, who was conducting the investigation, realized that one of the most valuable pieces of advice he could give was that the authorities should pay special attention to the difficulties and pitfalls in the job which had caused previous employees to be unsatisfactory, and to make sure that each accepted candidate would be capable of overcoming these difficulties. During the Second World War an American investigator named J. C. Flanagan applied similar principles to the selection of staff undertaking managerial duties in the US Navy. Since that time this sort of approach has been called 'the critical incident approach', although the technique developed by Flanagan and given this name was of a statistical nature, taking into account the frequency of different types of incident.

The study of critical incidents provides an efficient way of making use of past experience. Apart from its use in selection, where we can make sure that we do not select staff who are going to repeat the failures of the past, critical incidents can be utilized whenever we are trying to devise a new scheme or system to replace an old one. Someone designing a training course could be well advised to think over the mistakes that people make and make sure that the new course trains people to avoid them. When someone is designing a new machine it will pay him to think about the defects in the old machine and make sure that these are not repeated in the new one. When planning a holiday, or buying a house or looking for a new job, it is common sense to think of critical aspects of what one had before, but nevertheless it is surprising how many times the mistakes of the past are repeated in the present. Presumably it is because we are creatures of habit and our bad habits persist just as readily as our good ones.

LISTING

If we are seeking ideas related to a particular topic we can decide to write them down as a list. We may decide upon a particular number of ideas that we are going to try to collect or we may wish to think of everything that will be needed for some purpose. In either case the mind can usually carry out a search of relevant ideas stored in memory and produce with little difficulty a series of suitable items to complete the list.

Listing involves the same sort of mental process as actually going round looking for the real thing we want, but the effect of searching in a field of mental images is quite different from the effect of searching in a field of real things. Consider, for example, the difference between what we would put in a shopping list and what we would actually buy if we went straight to a shop without making a list. The visit to the shop might well be more stimulating than just thinking about what to buy, but making a list might more accurately meet our real needs.

ARTIFICIALLY BRINGING DIFFERENT IDEAS INTO CONJUNCTION

Our minds have a remarkable facility of being able to derive further ideas from the comparison of one idea with another. Imagination and intelligence which contribute to this mental skill will always vary considerably from one person to another, but there are several ways in which we can deliberately aid and exploit the creative properties of the mind by artificially bringing ideas into conjunction. By doing so we can arrange for the mind to be provided with an unlimited supply of 'food for thought'.

The most natural way to ensure that we are brought up against fresh ideas is to get into contact with other thinking people. We can do this by attending lectures, conferences, courses of training, clubs, and suchlike, where we know that other people are going to talk about subjects which interest us, or we can approach friends and colleagues about our problems and enlist their co-operation.

Strangely enough, we can often get inspiration from discussions in which we are not particularly involved. Somehow even when we are getting bored, we can start playing about with a thought set off by the present circumstances, and turn it into something that can be usefully applied to a more interesting situation elsewhere. For example, I once went to hear a public lecture. I can recall nothing whatever of what the well-known speaker said, but I shall never forget the example of first-rate chairmanship provided by the chairman of the meeting, whom I have ever since tried to emulate when required to act as chairman myself.

RANDOM STARTERS

This is a method that I discovered almost by accident during a teaching session with a group of managers, when I was trying to explain how readily common objects which lie around us can be used as sources of ideas. I decided to ask everybody in the group to look around in the room where we were working, to let his gaze alight on any randomly chosen object and then to write down a word or two to identify it. I next asked each person to think of a task he had to perform or a problem he had to solve and then to try to find a way of relating the object to the task or problem so as to suggest a useful way of tackling it. The results of this experiment were remarkable, because every member was able to carry out the instructions easily and without hesitation. One was able to relate a pot of paste that he had noticed in the room to his problem of writing a report. He realized that he could compose the report by pasting together bits of writing that he had already prepared. Another member of the group looked at a drinking glass and related it to a talk that he was preparing. He saw in it the need to be 'transparent', in the sense of speaking sincerely and frankly so that he would be able to communicate something of himself as a person to his audience.

I have since used this method successfully on many occasions and now regard it as one of the simplest yet most powerful. The way it seems to work is to provide a starting point for a chain of ideas which extends by association away from the starting object until it becomes within 'thinking distance' of the task or problem, whereupon a further idea is produced which links the task or problem to the nearest point of the train of ideas and completes the connection. Sometimes the final linking idea is a well known idea which this method merely reminds us of, but at other times it may be an idea of considerable originality which could not readily have been reached by any other route.

ATTRIBUTE LISTING

This technique was originated by Professor Robert Crawford of the University of Nebraska. As the name suggests, it is based upon the preparation of a list of the attributes of some chosen article.

It is frequently used to generate ideas for a new product, and the result can sometimes bear only a distant resemblance to the article used as the source of ideas.

Suppose, for example, that we choose a suitcase as the article to start from. What are the attributes of the particular suitcase that we have in mind? There is one near me as I write. Here is my list of its attributes.

1. Covered in grey plastic material.
2. Soft top.
3. Fibreglass frame.
4. Chromium-plated locks.
5. Expandable metal locks and hinges.
6. Two locks, two hinges.
7. Plastic-coated handle.
8. Tapes inside to restrain clothes.
9. Locks which open with the same key as that supplied with many similar cases.
10. Rounded corners.
11. It has a certain size . . .
12. It has a certain shape . . .
13. The interior is lined with soft cloth and there are some pockets.

The next step is to take each attribute in turn and alter it deliberately, to see what happens. Firstly, what would happen if we were to make a suitcase covered in some other material? What else could be used? Leather, metal, wood, canvas, fur, rubber, foam plastic, slats, embroidery, carpet, paper, buttons, beads, paint, photographs, anything we please. Immediately it can be seen that we have touched upon the idea of a range of decorative suitcases, a suggestion which has some novelty and could quite easily be put into practice.

Clearly, the same sort of treatment could be given to any of the other attributes. Let us briefly examine the locks in greater detail.

Locks 1. Two in number.
2. One key for both.
3. Key can be lost.
4. They have gone rusty.
5. Locks fitted to outside of body of case, clasps fitted to outside of lid.
6. They fasten outside the case.

There is no overwhelming reason why the locks should not be on the inside of the case, or indeed in between, where the lid overlaps the body of the case, which could make them less conspicuous and give them better protection from damage and rust.

MORPHOLOGICAL ANALYSIS

One of the more elaborate schemes for artificially bringing ideas into conjunction is the method of 'morphological analysis', which was devised by Dr. F. Zwicky and has been used with spectacular success in ventures such as the Apollo space project.

Its primary purpose is to help designers to invent new products and new ways of doing things. It leads anyone who uses it to consider a whole field of new possibilities which would otherwise be beyond the scope of his unaided imagination. Its name may be somewhat forbidding, but we should not allow that to put us off from making its acquaintance.

Morphological analysis can be used when we are deliberately seeking novelty in a particular field of interest. Suppose that we have set ourselves the object of devising a new game that we would like to manufacture and sell. We first set about analysing the characteristics of games. What does a game consist of? Well, lots of things. Let us put them down in the form of a list, and include the characteristics of any games we can think of.

Characteristics of some games

>Equipment
>An element of chance
>A ball
>Aiming at a target
>Quietness or noisiness
>Number of players, as teams or individuals
>Restfulness or strenuousness
>Suitability for young or old.

Having recognized these characteristics, the next step is to draw up a list or table of all the possible combinations that can be made from them. Thus, one possible combination would be a team game for six players which is a noisy but restful game of chance suitable for the young. The characteristics fall into groups of alternatives, and the total number of possible arrangements is the product of all the numbers of alternatives in the groups. What this procedure does, in effect, is to generate a large number of specifications which we may consider.

The next step is to work through the whole set, trying to devise for each combination of attributes a game which meets that particular specification. The hope is that among the large number of possible solutions there will be at least one worth going ahead with and eventually manufacturing and putting on the market.

THE ART OF INDICATION

The great Francis Bacon was a prolific creator of new ideas. No doubt he was a man of outstanding intelligence and imagination, but he was also an enthusiastic user of idea-generating techniques. One that he wrote about extensively was called the 'art of indication'. By this he meant the art of using the experience we have gained in doing one thing to indicate something similar that might be worth trying out. If paper can be made out of linen, he said, let us see what happens if we try to make it out of silk or hair or cotton or skins, even though these materials do not seem at first glance to be quite right for the purpose.

This principle has been extended by modern writers and is reflected, for example, in some of the questioning techniques mentioned earlier and in morphological analysis. Bacon also developed it in another direction to become the basis of inductive logic, the process by which general ideas are derived from accumulated experience.

Here is a practical and modern example of the art of indication. A manager who was responsible for the up-dating and production of large-scale maps was in difficulty because of a shortage of draughtsmen of the very high standard of skill required. At that time there was no shortage of draughts-men of normal skill as employed on less exacting work. The manager was acquainted with the processes of photography, and he remembered that when a photograph is reduced in size it gains in detail and sharpness. He realized that it was possible to make use of this fact by transferring it from the realm of photography to the realm of cartography. Then he was able to have alterations to maps drawn on extra large scale by the draughtsmen available to him and have them reduced photographically. The reduced photographs were overlaid on the maps where alterations were needed and the whole was then re-printed. In this way the obstacle of shortage of skilled staff was overcome without losing quality in the product.

THE ESSAY TRICK

A very effective method which can be used for writing essays, compositions or stories, particularly those we are encouraged to write when we are learning foreign languages, is to make use of a book of idioms or phrases. If we write down the title of the essay and then start to read through the book we shall soon come across an idiom that seems to bear some sort of relationship to the title of the essay. We can then write it down and proceed to look further. Soon we may find another idiom which attracts our attention, either because it also relates to the title, or else because it has a connection with the first idiom that we chose. One idea will lead to another, and we shall soon have a list of a dozen or so useful and strongly inter-related words and phrases. Contemplation of the list, helped by reading it through several times, will generate several more ideas of our own, and before we know where we are we have filled the list out into a connected theme. This will only require the addition of some linking parts of speech from our existing vocabulary to string it together to form a complete composition. The result will have originality and literary style and will give a very strong impression of linguistic competence. I know that this can be done, because I used to do it successfully when I was at school, and I have told many others how to do it.

Now, if this device were only applicable to writing essays at school it would not merit a place in this book, because our purpose is more serious than that. The real reason for its inclusion is its applicability to more general classes of problem.

If, for example, we are writing an article, we may start by piecing together fragments collected from a file of newspaper cuttings. If we are furnishing a new house or a new office we may start by putting together ideas or pictures collected from magazines, catalogues and advertisements. If we are seeking ideas for a meal we may get them from a look around the larder or the supermarket. Composers of all periods have taken inspiration from haphazard patterns of sound and turned them into music, and painters have done the same with accidental patterns of shape and colour.

JUNK MODELS

This technique was used by famous landscape painters of the past when they were devising new pictorial compositions. By putting together pieces of stone, wood, twigs, and various odds and ends they created a scaled-down model of a hypothetical landscape, which they were able to embellish with realistic details and then use as the basis of sketches which led eventually to the production of a full-scale studio painting. This method can be applied not only to artistic purposes but also to design problems such as the layout of workplaces and factories. For example, when some men were trying to design a dish-washing machine which could be lifted in and out of a kitchen sink, they found some boxes lying around to experiment with. They used one box to represent the machine and the other the sink, and were able to find out more about whether or not their ideas would work in practice.

THE MIND'S NATURAL TENDENCY TO EXPLORE THE UNKNOWN AND COMPLETE THE INCOMPLETE

When the mind receives a message which is different from what we are expecting, or is incomplete, or appears to be so, unconscious processes will either alter the message to make it nearer to what was expected, or else will give rise to curiosity about what is missing.

For example, if we are reading a sentence in a book without too much care and our eyes and their associated mental apparatus do not receive the whole message clearly, the mind may take the initiative and complete the sentence by inserting a word or two which it thinks is appropriate, thereby causing us to receive in consciousness a quite erroneous impression of what is actually there. On the other hand, if a page is missing in a book it is likely that we shall become very curious to know what was written on it. If our attention is drawn to a person who is facing away from us we may either make an assumption about what his face looks like or we may develop a wish to go and look at his face. Sometimes both reactions occur together.

It was the desire not to leave a gap in their understanding which led thinkers of olden times to invent myths in order to explain obscure natural phenomena. Today scientists are driven by the same forces of curiosity to find out more and more about the nature of the universe as a whole and every part and aspect of it.

Some people are more highly motivated to fill up the gaps than others. We have all met people who are so intolerant of gaps that if we are speaking to them and have to pause for an instant in order to think of a word, they will supply one for us, free, gratis, and for nothing. Although the word may fit the sense of the sentence it is not usually what we want to say, especially if we are trying to tell them something interesting.

The following techniques are based on these mental characteristics.

SKETCHING

Sketching, in the sense of making an initial attempt to express what something is going to look like, helps very effectively to turn rough ideas into practicable plans. Lines and marks on paper suggest real forms and relationships. A vague idea turns into something more definite in the very act of sketching. A rough sketch leads to a more finished sketch and eventually to a complete picture. But sketching takes place in a figurative sense as well as a literal one. Any kind of representation of an idea in thought or words or symbols can be started off in a rough or sketchy form, so that it can be recorded, examined, and thought about further. The sketch is an incomplete stage in working out an idea, and its very incompleteness serves as a mental challenge to take it through to a satisfactory stage of completion.

It is much easier to improve and build upon an idea that has already been expressed than to produce a good idea right from the beginning. Therefore, to produce a tentative suggestion as to what might be done to solve a problem is like throwing a line over a chasm that has to be bridged. Even though it may be neither strong nor firm it can be used to pull across other things from which a permanent bridge can be constructed. When two or more people are working together on a problem, it is helpful if one will put up a preliminary proposal and let others take what is of most use in it and contribute their own improvements and additions and so on until a complete solution has been put together. The one who puts up the first rough idea must be prepared for it to be treated without too much respect. He can make it clear to his colleagues that his suggestion is merely a sketch or a cock-shy, and they will understand that they are expected to regard it as no more than a starting point for further thinking.

CROSS-FERTILIZATION

When a number of people are working together the process of 'cross-fertilization' can take place, by which better ideas are produced through the interaction of the contributions of different people. This operates by the stimulating effect of new ideas and by trying out new points of view. Sometimes, as in the art of indication, the principles which helped to solve a problem in one situation can be recognized and transferred effectively to a quite different situation. An example of this occurred when the manager of a very productive coal-mine was talking about his methods of leadership. The manager of a public relations department took part in this discussion and realized that he could adapt some of these successful methods in his own field of work, even though it was so different from coal-mining.

Experience shows that the cross-fertilization of ideas does not take place as often as it might. We are often too jealous of our own ideas and we do not take up the opportunities for productive interchange which occur.

The way to improve our use of cross-fertilization is to spend more time discussing the constructive stage of solving a problem with other people. When we do this we should spend at least as much time in listening as in talking; unless we are good listeners the seed will not stay long enough to germinate.

CHAIN REACTIONS

In certain circumstances the effects of the cross-fertilization of ideas can be extremely powerful. When a striking idea is brought to the attention of someone who is both receptive and enthusiastic he can be so strongly stimulated by it that he is propelled into action, and may develop a further idea which affects a third person in a similar fashion. A train of causes and effects can be set up in this way and may persist for some time, changing its form and direction at each meeting of minds, but continuing the chain reaction as long as the force of the impact of each new idea is above a critical level. Here is a simple but fascinating example of such a chain. A person who was enthusiastic about making small knitted toys in the shape of animals wrote an article on the subject for a magazine. A girl read the article and became interested, and persuaded her mother to help her to make a number of the toys to sell at a charity fete. A man saw the attractive toys and bought one. Not having any use for it himself, he thought of the idea of sending it to a relative as a joke and wrote a humorous letter to go with it, pretending to explain how the toy animal came into his possession. The relative received the toy animal and letter at a time when she was preparing a talk on the subject of humour, and decided to use them as illustrative material in the talk. The talk was a huge success; some of the audience became so enthusiastic that they gave presents to the speaker and some declared their resolve to try to find ways of bringing more humour into their lives. What happened next in this chain is at present unrecorded, but who knows, it may still be continuing and there may yet be further repercussions taking place in different shapes and forms.

Although it can hardly be claimed that this type of chain reaction can be put to practical use when trying to solve an ordinary problem, at least it suggests what to do when we have an exciting new idea and don't know how to put it into effect—give it away to someone else who can use it!

SIMULATING

Most of our problems arise out of familiar situations and are solved quickly because there are many clues pointing to courses of action known to be effective. However, from time to time we have to face up to problems where clues are lacking or where we lack experience or knowledge of appropriate courses of action. In these instances the way forward may be to create an artificial situation which simulates the real situation. In this way we can create pertinent clues or experience which we did not possess previously.

The processes of sketching and of making junk models, which we have considered from other points of view, are both ways in which we can simulate experience and learn more about a problem. Supposing that we are going to make a piece of furniture, a stool, for example. The process of sketching it or making a rough model from junk, gives us an advance experience of some aspects of constructing it. We are stimulated to foresee problems that could arise in construction. When we get to the stages in construction where the problems actually occur, we know what to expect and we know much better what to do.

Making a more realistic model of a problem-situation may produce even more of this creative effect. Something that we can see and handle is easier to think about and more stimulating to creative thought than an abstract representation.

In situations where there is much at stake such as the design of aeroplanes, for example, it is inconceivable that a design could be completed without progressing through a number of stages of model-making. However, there are all kinds of problems which can benefit from the stimulating effect of modelling when courses of action are being constructed. We know that the police reconstruct a crime in order to get as close as they can to experiencing the actual events that occurred. Practising and rehearsing our parts in human situations at work and at home is something that we should consider seriously when a difficult or important occasion is approaching.

When it is not convenient to make a realistic model of a situation it is usually still possible to make one in symbolic form. Symbolic models of situations are often called games, such as war games and business games, both of which are used to stimulate creative thought and to provide vicarious experience. The name 'game' is appropriate because real games, especially those played spontaneously by children, serve an educative purpose. They stimulate the imagination and give an opportunity to try to solve problems which are relevant to important situations in life.

Even when we have no opportunity to do anything practical that will simulate a situation, we can at least think about it and go through the anticipated or reconstructed events in the mind's eye. We can imagine what it would be like, and try to complete the mental pictures that come to us. One of the functions of dreams and daydreams seems to be to provide an opportunity for the rehearsal of actual or foreseeable experiences that we believe to be problematical. Dreams are not something that we can produce deliberately to help in our creative work, but we ought to be able to find time now and then for meditating about the situations for which we are seeking new ideas.

GAP-FILLING

In order to exploit the mind's ability to fill the gap between parts of an incomplete answer to a problem we can make a point of highlighting the place where the gap occurs, the place where the missing link needs to be inserted. This is one of the main tasks facing the chairman of a meeting which has been convened in order to solve a problem. If he can describe to the meeting exactly what needs to be done and persuade all of the members that it is their business to discover how to do it, then he will have done a great deal to ensure that the work of the meeting will be productive. We are doing precisely the same thing when we take care to identify and define a problem in terms of an objective and the obstacle which prevents us from reaching it. This process helps the mind to carry out its gap-filling function by focusing attention on the point where creative thought is required.

TWISTING

When we are looking for ideas to meet a particular objective, we may come up with some suggestions which are nearly right but are lacking in some respects. It is remarkable how easy it is to modify or 'twist' such an idea and convert it into the kind of idea that we want. As was mentioned in the description of 'brainstorming', even an unlikely suggestion or 'wild idea' about how the problem might be solved can be chosen and 'twisted' to make it into something really useful. In a few moments someone can usually produce a variant of the 'wild idea' that will be of considerable value. In an actual brainstorming session on the subject of 'how to make ourselves more decisive', someone in the throes of 'free-wheeling' once suggested that we should all have compulsory siestas at work. When this gem was subjected to the process of twisting it took only a few seconds for another person to transform it into the eminently sensible idea that we should make sure that we deal with important decisions while we are fresh and not put them off until we have become tired and the ability to make up our minds has deteriorated.

Another example occurred when we were 'brainstorming' a military problem on the subject of how to get a damaged tank out of a bog. 'Blow up the tank' was the wildest idea we found and this was quickly twisted into two useful ideas. The first was to provide an inflatable bag which could be 'blown up', in the other sense of the expression, in order to push the tank upwards. The second was to make an explosion beside the tank to compact the material of the bog and create a ramp up which the tank could be towed or driven.

As long as we are quite clear what sort of ideas we need, we can take any idea whatsoever and give it a twist in the right direction. This is the way that many jokes are invented or adapted to fit particular situations. If we are going to give a talk to some salesmen and we know a joke about public relations men, we may be able to alter the characters to fit our audience. It is often possible to make a joke based on a picture hanging in the room where we are going to make a speech. We can twist the meaning of the picture to contrast with the theme of the talk, or we can pretend that a portrait on view depicts a notable member of the audience and cause it to be laughed at as a caricature.

TEACHING

It is well known that one of the best ways of forcing our ideas into good order is to do some teaching in the subject concerned. This not only does wonders for our understanding of the subject but also enables us to see things in a new light, which often leads through to new insights and new discoveries. Part of this benefit comes from the work of preparation, but much of it also comes from interaction between the teacher and his class, which shows up differences of viewpoint needing to be resolved. Opportunities to teach are not exclusive to members of the teaching profession. In the family, at work, and in social life we can benefit from being alert to situations in which we can teach and learn from each other. While Jakow Trachtenberg was in a concentration camp during the Second World War he taught himself how to solve all kinds of mental arithmetic problems systematically. He had no tutor, no textbooks, and almost no writing materials for recording his discoveries. Nevertheless he produced an astonishing amount of new ideas on the subject, which are available to us all in a book called *The Trachtenberg Speed System of Basic Mathematics*, translated by A. Cutler and R. McShane.

LATERAL THINKING

I am sometimes asked for my views about the relationship between 'lateral thinking', the concept originated by Edward de Bono, and the methods described in this chapter. 'Lateral thinking' seems to be founded on the idea of a distinction between straightforward thinking and thinking which deliberately avoids the direct path, but I have found that in practice this distinction is more difficult to make than would appear at first sight.

In Chapter 2 I quoted an example about a man who bought a roller-blind and found that it was too long to fit his window. He told me that his idea of drilling a hole in the wall to make more space for the roller was the result of 'lateral thinking', but he came to realize later that the same process of thought could just as truly be described as a straightforward deduction from the facts of the situation.

However, I believe that if ordinary and apparently straightforward lines of thought do not yield the ideas we need to solve a problem a wider range of alternatives should be explored, and in trying to reach them the methods which enable us to break away from conventional patterns of thought are particularly likely to be helpful.

SUMMARY

If we need help in producing ideas for solving a problem there are methods available to enhance our natural creative abilities. The four principles of freeing the mind of inhibiting influences, utilizing past experience, artificially bringing different ideas into conjunction, and using the mind's natural tendency to explore the unknown and complete the incomplete, can each be applied in a number of different ways. The choice of method depends upon the nature of the problem and the needs and inclinations of the problem-solver.

EXERCISES

1. Go through the list of techniques described in this chapter and apply each one to a creative problem of your choice. Make a note of your achievements and try to find out which techniques help you most.
2. Design a new type of kitchen gadget.
3. Invent a plot for a new play.
4. Invent a plot for a novel.
5. Draw an abstract picture by superimposing the shapes of a few objects available to you.
6. Design a new kind of pencil-sharpener. Do not forget to begin by stating and analysing your definition of the problem.
7. The next time you take part in a discussion, count the number of critical remarks made and observe their effect on the people to whom they were addressed. Did criticism tend to stimulate or to inhibit?
8. Devise a set of questions for the purpose of getting people to think of better methods of educating children than those currently used in schools. Try the questions on yourself first and then on one or two other people. Observe whether the answers were appropriate to the questions or not and try to account for any discrepancies.
9. Take any book and select ten words from it by an arbitrary method. One way to do this is to take (say) the last word on the fourth line of any ten pages. Now make up a sentence or two which brings in all ten words. This is a good exercise in verbal ingenuity and can be made easier or harder by adjusting the number of given words. It can be used as a game to pass the time away on journeys.
10. Take ten or so randomly chosen words and use any ideas that they may suggest as the basis of a short story. Write the story out in full.

11. Make a list of six things that you need. Reconsider each item and make sure that you really do need it. Then devise several courses of action that could help you to satisfy each need, using suitable methods from this chapter to help in the generation of ideas.

12. Having done exercise 11 for yourself, do the same for somebody else.

10

Building the Bridge of Ideas

Problems can be very daunting when they require a large collection of ideas to be put together. Many people feel that they would like to write a book at some time during their lives, but when they start thinking about the magnitude of the task they get 'cold feet' and never get started. Having to write a report, prepare a speech or organize some complex activity can be equally off-putting. Probably the main reason for this kind of apprehension is that we know that if we tried to do any of these things straight off we would be very likely to make a hash of it. This is an understandable attitude, but it is not a wise one because there are other ways of going about such a task which are easier and more effective.

To solve the problem we have to build a bridge of ideas. It must be capable of fitting the situation in which we now are, where we have the problem, and it must be able to carry us over to the situation that we are trying to get to where our objective will have been achieved. The bridge must fit at both ends, it must lie in the right direction, it must be continuous, and it must extend far enough to reach right across.

We have already a good deal of knowledge about what needs to be done and we can see where further knowledge is going to come from. We know how to make the bridge of ideas fit at both ends from our clear definition of the problem and our analysis of the situation. We have a general sense of direction based upon our understanding and interpretation of

147

the problem. Our actual line of construction, which will be the main guide, will be derived from our strategic plans regarding the objective and the obstacle. The continuity and satisfactory extent of our ideas will depend upon the ideas themselves, which will have to be selected and shaped so that they join up to each other accurately. Where there are gaps these will have to be filled in.

Here is an example showing how the bridge of ideas has to be made to fit 'State A' and 'State B' and form a continuous link between them.

The problem was that an old lady (an invalid, but not the one mentioned before) was in the habit of getting out of bed

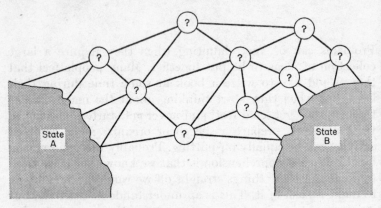

FIGURE 8.   The bridge of ideas

in the middle of the night and causing a certain amount of havoc. The objective was to bring about a new situation in which any movement of the invalid would be detected as soon as possible and brought to the attention of her daughter who looked after her. The obstacle was that there was no channel of communication between the old lady and her daughter at night-time. The strategy decided upon was to provide a suitable channel of communication.

The first course of action that was proposed was to provide an electric bell. An electric bell should have been capable of alerting the daughter and informing her that the invalid required attention. The electric bell therefore fitted 'State B', the state of affairs prevailing once the objective had been reached. The idea of the electric bell was not sufficient on its own to solve the problem, because the bell would not ring of itself at the right time. It was not adapted to 'State A'. Nevertheless, there was nothing against this idea and no reason to reject it. In looking for a way to fit this idea to 'State A', it was natural to think of giving the invalid a bell-push and to complete the bridge of ideas by providing an electrical circuit by means of a battery and interconnecting wires. This would produce a channel of information connecting the patient and bell-push via the wires and battery to the electric bell at the bedside of her daughter.

Unfortunately, this course of action did not produce the desired result. Although the invalid was strong enough to operate the bell-push she found it difficult and for one reason or another was disinclined to use it. Therefore the bell did not ring when the invalid was about to get out of bed.

A second course of action was therefore devised. The electric bell, well adapted to 'State B', was retained. The idea of using a photo-electric cell to detect the patient's movement in getting out of bed was considered. A photo-electric cell fitted 'State A' no better than a bell-push, because the invalid could not by herself operate a photo-electric cell. However, it was realized that if a beam of light were directed above the invalid as she lay in bed, any movement of hers in attempting to sit up in order to get out of bed would interrupt the beam of light. This would alter the electrical resistance of the photo-electric cell and this effect could be made to operate the electric bell through the agency of an amplifier and relay. This solution was put into effect and was found to be satisfactory.

WHERE TO START BUILDING IDEAS

It is natural to choose a starting point where we are now. Certainly the ideas that we seek must be adapted to fit our present circumstances, for otherwise they will not be prac-ticable. If, for example, we are planning to re-decorate our bedroom, we must take account of the present size and shape of the bedroom, the furniture we possess, the amount of money we have to spend, our own skill at painting and decorating and so on. A teacher has to consider the capabilities and present knowledge and state of mind of his students before he can successfully think out what to do in order to achieve certain educational objectives. A manager should consider the attitudes and habits of his employees before making changes.

Although these matters have to be considered at some stage, they are not always the best ones to think about first. The danger is that our thoughts may be led off in the wrong direction. Generally speaking, the soundest way to begin is to consider the end-state first and work backwards to find out what intermediate points will have to be passed. If we understand what our objective really implies, we can usually recognize that certain principles must be followed if it is to be attained satisfactorily. These principles are not separate from the main objective itself but are essential requirements for its achievement.

Principles of this kind give direction to our creative thinking by showing what kinds of ideas are needed and help us to avoid planning unsatisfactory courses of action. However, it is not always easy to get the principles right in the first instance, and therefore we should try them out as early as possible so that we have a chance to make corrections before we have invested too much time and effort in our creative thinking.

It is surprising and somewhat disappointing to find that committees of inquiry and other official commissions set up by the Government to look into important national questions do not always begin their investigations by working out a set of principles to which their findings should conform. From time to time, however, one finds clear evidence that an inquiry has been conducted in an eminently methodical manner. An admirable example is to be seen in the *Report of the Committee of Inquiry on Decimal Currency* which was published in September 1963. I give a full quotation of the first four sections of Chapter II as a lesson in clear thinking and a demonstration of how it is possible to state one's principles at the very beginning.

CHAPTER II

CHOICE OF DECIMAL SYSTEM: GENERAL PRINCIPLES

General

23. This chapter describes the general principles which guided our search for a suitable decimal currency for the United Kingdom and lists some of the questions which had to be answered before our choice could be made.

24. There are some features which logic and the experience of other countries suggest should be incorporated, or avoided, in a good decimal currency if the advantages of decimalisation are to be gained. One of our main aims has been to embody these ideal features in the currency we recommend. But it is not possible to apply abstract criteria to determine the precise value of currency units and, in designing a decimal currency, this presents more problems than determining the relationship of units one with another. Because of this, and because changing our currency would be an enterprise likely to find greater public acceptance if the new system had points of obvious contact with the old, there is nothing to be gained, and much to be lost, by selecting a system in which the links with our present currency are slight. Inevitably, we had to consider ways of decimalising the existing currency, not of starting afresh with a completely new one, bearing no relationship to the old.

25. In the main, therefore, a decimal system to replace our present currency has to be judged by its relationship with £. s. d. This does not imply that we must select the system under which amounts can most readily be converted to and from sterling (a point we shall discuss in detail in Chapter VI) but that we must pick one which, so far as is consistent with incorporation of the ideal features, retains the best characteristics and associations of £. s. d. and minimises the difficulties, the public confusion, and the cost, of a transition to decimal working.

Desirable features

26. In our view eight features are desirable in a decimal currency system. They can be divided, as follows, into two groups of four, the first group being features inherent in the system, the second being features relating to the introduction of the system:

The system

   (*i*) should be a consistent decimal system and should seek to maximise the benefits hoped for from decimalisation;

   (*ii*) should be simple;

   (*iii*) should be flexible, and convenient for money transactions of all values;

   (*iv*) should be lasting.

The introduction of the system

   (*v*) should not affect the international standing of sterling;

   (*vi*) should not present people with undue difficulties of adaptation in the changeover period;

   (*vii*) should not result in avoidable price increases;

   (*viii*) should not result in unduly high machine and non-machine costs.

This chapter is concerned primarily with the four features in the first group.

BUILDING UP THE IDEAS

Once we have plotted out the general pattern or shape to which the bridge of ideas needs to conform, in terms of the end-states and connecting principles, the process of construction can begin.

A complex structure of ideas, such as a book, is hardly ever produced just by starting at the beginning and going onwards until the end is reached as in writing a letter to a friend or in playing a game of chess. A very experienced and fluent writer might plan the book as a whole on certain principles with a rough idea of how many chapters there will be and what will go into them, and then write large chunks of it until it is finished. But a less experienced and less fluent author would do better to fill in the details of his plan by working from several starting points at different times and building up a number of separate pieces of the book until they eventually meet. The starting points can be themes which the author has thought out analytically from a consideration of the objective that he is trying to achieve, or they can be sundry bits and pieces of material which he has gathered from time to time and odd ideas that have been noted down. The process of expanding such ideas into fuller notes or into finished prose may give rise to further ideas about the material required to fill in the gaps or about better ways of structuring the book in part or as a whole.

In writing this particular book I have been guided by the general strategy of producing five main sections on the five main stages of problem-solving, having collected over a period of several years a quantity of items to put in each one. Material which did not fit logically or conveniently into one of these sections has been found a place elsewhere or put aside for possible future use. When I was working on a particular section I had a list of topics beside me to remind me what was to go into it. After each piece had been written I gave it a name to identify it and wrote that down in a summary of the contents of the section to which it belonged. By this means, whenever I needed to refresh my memory of what had and had not been completed, I could quickly review everything that I had written and see exactly where it fitted in.

In a large-scale project, such as designing a new factory, the possibility of working directly forward like writing a letter is quite out of the question because of the multi-dimensional nature of the problem. In such a case the detailed work can be built up around either the nucleus of ideas or instructions that we already possess, or around problem areas that we have identified as a result of analysing the situation. Work on the development of a particular idea may go on steadily until the part of the problem to which it belongs has been solved, or it may come to a halt because of some obstacle which has not yet been overcome. In the latter case it is usually advisable to drop that line of thought for the time being and take up some other issue which may be more likely to yield. In an examination, for example, it is always best to do the easy questions first, to make sure of them, and then use any remaining time on the harder ones which by that time, through the process of incubation, we may be able to understand and answer more satisfactorily.

The piecemeal approach we have been advocating here is usually more adaptable and flexible than the direct-line approach that one might otherwise try to pursue. This is because the separate parts under development can be altered at will and at any time, like an oil painting which can be scraped off or overpainted as the artist makes his mind up about the content of the picture. If we complete each part in strict sequence there is a risk of having to make big revisions and go back over several parts if unexpected changes need to be made towards the end. The development of the set of ideas as an integrated whole can be supervised more easily if the parts come on together than if they are dealt with one at a time, just as children of similar ages usually grow up better as a family than children greatly separated in age.

CONTROLLING THE DIRECTION OF IDEAS

No matter how well we have done our preparatory thinking, there still remains the need to know whether or not our ideas lead along the line that we intended to follow and whether this line is still going to get us to our objective. The clearest examples of this need are those in which the problem is handed over from one person to another to solve; when someone is given instructions to carry out a task it is unlikely that it will be done exactly as the originator of the idea intended. This is partly because the originator fails to give regard to the eventualities that may occur on the way and partly because the other person is influenced by his own interpretation of what the situation requires.

Similar risks arise in the posing and answering of questions. A question embodies a specification for some requested ideas. The answer is an attempt to meet the specification. When the answer is unsatisfactory, this is either because the question did not convey the questioner's meaning accurately, or because the respondent did not say what he was asked to say.

The examination questions we referred to come into this category, and many of us have experienced disasters where we strayed away from the real point of the question which the examiner asked. In business or politics, where there may be much at stake and little opportunity to correct errors, this can be a most serious matter. The need for care is obvious, but the need to check-up on the reaction of other people concerned is often overlooked. In conversation it is useful to put in such remarks as 'Do you follow?' 'Does that make sense to you?' 'Have I understood you?' 'Is that what you mean?' in order to find out whether the other party is 'on the same wavelength' as ourselves. If we are trying to persuade someone to agree to our wishes and we see that a particular line of argument is not getting anywhere it is best to stop, because the other person will not appreciate having his time wasted and being denied the chance to express his own views.

A book is rather a one-way form of communication and the author has to wait a long time to get a reaction to his words. He can try out sections of the manuscript on his friends and relations as the writing proceeds, but what matters is the whole book and the reactions of his readers to it. As for myself, I would be most grateful to any reader who would be so kind as to tell me his views about this book, especially if he can identify any further areas of the subject of problem-solving where methods need to be developed.

In some fields we have been taught or have learnt by experience how to steer our way towards a solution of the problem. A tailor takes a prescribed set of measurements of his customer before he begins to work on a suit of clothes, and as the work progresses he arranges one or more fittings in order to make fine adjustments and ensure that the suit will conform accurately to the shape and size of the customer's body. When someone is cooking the dinner they look in the oven once or twice to see how the roasting of the joint is progressing. They adjust the temperature so that the meat will be ready at the right time. Examples of routine problems are plentiful and familiar, but our main interest in this chapter is the creative approach required for problems where there is not a readily available answer.

The only way we can tell whether creative work is proceeding in the right direction is to find out whether or not the ideas being put forward are consistent with the principles that we have decided to follow. But it is difficult to make an accurate evaluation of an incomplete course of action. If we are considering a single idea related to the solution of the problem we are quite likely to be biased in our judgement of it simply because, as it stands, it is incapable of solving the problem; it has all the appearance of a 'half-baked idea'. When we listen to the discussion of a group of people trying to devise a course of action we often hear useful ideas being rejected by sceptics who do not appreciate the value of the contributions because they cannot imagine how they could work out in practice. They see the possibility of failure, but not the likelihood of success. An incomplete idea is very difficult to defend in a discussion with other people when they are in a sceptical or critical mood. For these reasons it is much better to work out the set of ideas to a degree of finality before judging them.

MAKING PROGRESS

Making progress is not the same as controlling the direction of the development of ideas. Progress is more a matter of speed, whereas direction is more a matter of accuracy. However, there is always a relationship between speed and accuracy, because an increase in speed will probably require the sacrifice of accuracy, and a loss of accuracy which has to be rectified will lead to a loss of speed.

It is a curious thing that when we are working with ideas we are often careless about the amount of progress we are making. Our discussions are allowed to wander from the point at issue, we get lost in thought, or we become distracted by red herrings. One wonders why this should be because it is very wasteful, yet some people are always complaining that they do not have enough time to think.

This is probably best regarded as a matter of motivation rather than self-discipline or conscientiousness. When we feel that it is important to make progress we work harder and are more careful to avoid getting side-tracked. Personally, I find I cannot concentrate by an effort of will, but if I am interested enough in my task I cannot avoid concentrating on it.

TEST OF COMPLETION

The constructive stage of problem-solving is complete when we possess one or more courses of action which we believe to be capable of reaching the objective and of dealing satisfactorily with the obstacle. We have then gone far enough to proceed to the next stage of decision-making.

SUMMARY

The course of action we adopt to solve a problem must be appropriate to present circumstances as well as to the end result we are trying to achieve. Therefore our task is to find out what is needed to meet these requirements and to build a bridge which joins the beginning and end states together. The constructional work can be guided by principles worked out beforehand so that we may know what ideas to look for and how they should all fit together.

The constructional work can begin at either end or at different points in the strategic plan. As long as we know what we are doing it is better to push forward wherever progress is possible rather than stick to a rigid and arbitrary sequence which may occasionally come to a complete standstill.

EXERCISES

1. How should an architect make sure that he meets the wishes of his client?
2. How could you start up a private newspaper of your own?
3. If you were the managing director of a large business, how would you prevent industrial unrest?
4. A manager had a subordinate who was so helpful to other people by solving their problems that he never gave enough attention to his own work. What would you have done about it?
5. Obtain a notebook and start noting down promising ideas

which occur at odd moments. Read it monthly to see what action is required to put the ideas into practice to solve your current problems.

6. When you next have to write a letter or report, plan it in advance and tick off or amend the items in the plan as the writing progresses.
7. If you had to design a home for old people, what principles would you try to make your design conform to?
8. The next time you try to solve a problem, either by yourself or with other people, write down all the proposals made and review them afterwards to see which of them helped to make progress and which did not. Would it have been possible to tell at the time they were put forward which ideas would be helpful and which were not?
9. Which are more likely to succeed, courses of action which involve making big changes or courses of action which involve making small changes? Why?

Stage 4

DECISION-MAKING

Stage 4

DECISION-MAKING

II

A Strategic View of Decision-making

Decision-making is the most dramatic stage of problem-solving, where we commit ourselves to a course of action. What was originally a problem becomes transformed into a successful or an unsuccessful solution. Some authors regard decision-making as the essence of all problem-solving, and some who write in the field of management take the view that the primary task of any manager is to make decisions.

The amount of attention which ought to be given to decision-making varies from one problem to another. Some problems, as we noted in Chapter 4, are almost entirely a matter of decision-making and their other stages are not really difficult or problematic. More usually, one of the other stages is the difficult one and the making of the decision is relatively straightforward. For this reason it can be misleading to use the term decision-making to refer to the whole problem-solving process.

ROUTES TO DECISION-MAKING

We can find ourselves at the decision-making stage having come by any one of three different routes. The first of these is the route of methodical problem-solving, starting from the detection of the problem and its correct identification and definition, passing through the stage of interpreting the problem, and the stage of constructing suitable courses of action. This is the safest and, in the long run, most efficient route, because methodical problem-solving will not lead us to the decision-making stage until we know that we have at least one course of action capable of solving the problem satisfactorily. If we have more than one possible course of action we shall need to make up our minds which one we prefer. The five steps of decision-making described in Chapter 12 form a logical procedure for doing this.

The second route by which one can get to the decision-making stage is by taking the problem over from somebody else. Frequently it happens that we are presented with some alternative courses of action and it is then up to us to make the choice between them. This may be a trivial matter like choosing among the dishes on a menu, or it may be more serious like choosing a school to send one's child to or voting for a parliamentary candidate. This route is perfectly legitimate and proper. When it has been followed we can make the decision as if we had produced the given alternatives ourselves. But since we did not devise them, it is important to check that what is offered for choice is capable of solving the problem and that nothing better has been overlooked. Suppose a manager is offered two or three alternative plans by a subordinate and is to choose among them. Clearly he should make sure that the alternatives are all capable of meeting the known objectives before he attempts to make his choice, and he should check whether there are any further obvious possibilities. If the situation is unsatisfactory he needs to tell the other people concerned, so that either more problem-solving work can be done to get a better solution or else the objective itself can be reconsidered and modified to make it more readily achievable.

The third route to the decision-making stage is the direct route which omits the earlier stages of problem-solving more or less entirely. To take this route is usually asking for trouble because it leaves only past experience and intuition to rely upon, which are likely to be insufficient in all but the most routine and trivial of problem-situations. In spite of this risk, however, many important decisions are taken without sufficient preparation, and such are the causes of many of our troubles in all areas of public and private life. Carelessness in decision-making frequently leads to actions which do not serve a useful purpose or which leave important issues out of account, especially the human aspects.

It may help to avoid careless decision-making if we pause at this point to consider some of the forms of faulty behaviour that can give rise to it.

COMMON CAUSES OF CARELESS DECISION-MAKING

Lack of clear objectives
Inattention to earlier stages of problem-solving
Ignorance of better methods
Laziness
Complacency
Prejudice
Recency of similar problems
Over-reliance on past experience
Copying other people's decisions
Impulsive reactions to events
Irresponsible indulgence of whims and fancies
Pursuit of private or irrelevant objectives
Uncritical pursuit of the obvious
Taking the easy way out.

It can be seen that several of the items in this list are similar to the blocks to interpretation and to creativity which we noted in Chapters 5 and 9. We can begin to learn how to avoid them by looking back at bad decisions we may have made in the past and trying to identify any of the items on the list which may have had an effect upon them.

PREMATURE DECISIONS

One of the very worst kind of decision-making errors is to make a decision and announce it impulsively before relevant data about it have been gathered. For example, and this has happened more than once, it is sometimes decided in a large business to celebrate and reward long service by giving a valuable present to all those who have been employed for, say, twenty-five years. This decision is announced and then a list is made of all the employees who have completed or are about to complete twenty-five years of service. Then, what a surprise! There are found to be so many people eligible for the award that the firm come to realize that this is going to be very expensive. So they cut the cost and proceed to give cheap presents instead of valuable ones, and in the event this gives no pleasure to the recipients and in fact causes a considerable amount of disappointment and dissatisfaction. If only those in authority would allow enough time for proposals to be evaluated, such setbacks could be avoided.

THE CASE OF THE ONE AND ONLY PROPOSED COURSE OF ACTION

At a time when an acquaintance of mine was very young, he decided that he wanted to become a doctor. When he reached the age at which one has to decide what subjects to study in the later stages of school life, his decision remained the same. However, his parents became concerned about the matter and saw the situation as a problem, because they were not sure that the decision of a little boy could remain valid for the rest of his life, and they felt that other possibilities should be brought into consideration. What happened next was that the boy and his parents received the advice of specialists in vocational guidance. Considerable attempts were made to probe and test the boy's adherence to his ambition to become a doctor, but his mind was made up and his convictions were unshakable. In due course he went to medical school where he received distinctions, and subsequent events have shown that a medical career was indeed a most satisfactory choice for him.

This was a real-life example of the type of situation where only one course of action is under consideration. In such situations it is unwise to allow events to proceed without trying to widen out the field of choice. This action can be taken by challenging the uniqueness of the one and only course of action, by asking whether it is really good enough to go ahead with as it stands. A method of giving point to such questions is to set up any conceivable alternative and demand to know why it is unacceptable as a substitute for the favoured course of action. In the case described above it could have been asked, for example, 'Why do you not want to go in for engineering?' and this would have helped to open up discussion on the problem.

URGENT DECISIONS

From time to time situations arise in which there is genuinely no opportunity to be methodical in our problem-solving, such as when we have to make a sudden decision whilst playing a game, or when somebody puts a question to us in conversation. In these circumstances we have to rely largely on intuition and habit to get us through. Yet there is usually sufficient time, even if only a split second, to identify the type of decision with which we are faced. Here we must reduce the problem to the simplest and most elementary terms. If we can only afford to ask ourselves one question, let it be this: 'In this situation, is the most important issue to avoid failure or to go all out for success?' The answer will usually tell us immediately which way to jump!

Here is an example from real life. An airline duty officer had to decide what to say to the passengers when their flight was delayed. He said they would be delayed during the unloading of some cargo that had come in from another airport on the aircraft on which they were intended to embark. He explained that he had not been told that this cargo would have to be unloaded. This was not a good decision, although one can appreciate that it had to be made quickly. But there was time enough to think whether it was a 'success' or 'failure' type of decision. 'Success' would have been to cause the passengers to feel that the best had been done in the circumstances. 'Failure' would have been to cause the passengers to feel that a bad decision had been made. Because it gave the impression that a mistake had occurred, the duty officer should have kept to himself the fact that he had not been informed, even though he wanted to indicate that the delay was not his fault.

DECISIVENESS

The question of decisiveness has two main aspects, the quickness of decision and the firmness of commitment once the decision has been made. Neither is an end in itself, but each is a way of avoiding unnecessary trouble. Quickness avoids the cost, waste, frustration, and uncertainty of delaying implementation. Uncertainty over big issues like business mergers and reorganizations is contagious and can cause widespread paralysis in an organization. Firmness of commitment avoids hesitations and all the unfortunate consequences of wavering from one course of action to another.

The ability to judge the need for decisiveness grows with experience, but it is not usually difficult to see when an advantage can be gained by a quick and approximate decision rather than a slow accurate one. Anyone who is naturally hesitant in making decisions can reassure himself by recognizing that if he tries to be decisive he may gain respect for avoiding delay, and in the long run he will certainly gain useful skill in judgement.

How to be Decisive

Here is a list of points which if attended to will give improved ability to be decisive.

1. Take pride in being decisive.
2. Be alert for hesitation and when this occurs assess whether or not the possible cost of a wrong decision outweighs the advantages of a quick decision.
3. Take enough time over the earlier stages of problem-solving. Then decision-making will be a simpler matter.
4. Once the decision-making stage has been reached, concentrate on it—don't let it lie.
5. Follow a procedure—be less subjective about decision-making.
6. Recognize these causes of indecision:
   (*a*) Lack of clear formulation of the problem.
   (*b*) Lack of understanding of the problem-situation.
   (*c*) Inadequate courses of action.
   (*d*) Lack of method in decision-making.
   (*e*) Inadequate evaluation of alternatives—over- and under-estimation of advantages and disadvantages and risks involved.

(*f*) No real difference between courses of action or their values.
7. Remember that a silly question does not warrant a long investigation.

WHEN NOT TO BE DECISIVE

There are two sorts of occasion when it is definitely wrong to try to be decisive in the sense to which we have just referred. The less important of these is a situation where the problem can be expected to decline in importance if left alone for a while, either because the objective is obsolescent or because the potency of the obstacle is coming to an end. Some people have a flair for spotting such problems and knowing which ones to put 'on the shelf' and postpone until there is more time or other resources, or until the problem no longer exists.

Tasks set impulsively by other people often come into this category. If we believe that a task, such as to prepare a document containing certain detailed information, is not really worthwhile, it is reasonable to suppose that the person who set it might eventually come to the same conclusion. So if we wait for a period and find that no reminder is sent to us, then that may be the end of the matter.

Another typical situation arises when we are selling a house. Many people arrange for their house to be redecorated before a sale in order to make it look as attractive as possible. But this is a matter of taste, and tastes in decoration vary so much that one is just as likely to make the house less attractive to a prospective buyer as to make it more attractive to him. Many people who have just bought a house have it redecorated as soon as they possible can, so one might as well save the money and be prepared to offer a small allowance in the price to compensate for any noticeable deficiencies.

In my own experience the policy of procrastination has often been successful when I have unintentionally agreed to attend two different functions or meetings at the same time. Rather than upset a number of people by asking for a change of date, I have left it for a while and then found that others have arranged a postponement or cancellation and solved the problem for me.

The other and more important type of situation is where there is much at stake and a rash decision could cause a serious error to be made. This is not such a matter of judgement as of prudence and of remembering to assess the seriousness of possible errors before rushing headlong into a decision.

I have had several experiences of this class of problem, in which another person has created serious difficulties for me in carrying out a task and I have been on the brink of a potentially disastrous confrontation with him. When I have been able to hold myself in check and deliberately turned my attention to other tasks it has usually turned out that my opponent had removed himself before long or has been removed by other circumstances, and I have then been able to make my way forward again without hindrance.

This example illustrates the advantage of maintaining a flexible approach and keeping open a wide range of options so that when one way forward is barred, progress can still be made in various other directions.

THERE IS NO RIGHT OR WRONG WAY TO MAKE A DECISION

In all this discussion of decision-making it is easy to overlook the fact that nobody can tell another person exactly how he should make a decision. The decision-maker has to take himself into account. Only he knows the truth about the personal values to be put into the equation. In other words, in making any practical decision there may be an ethical or moral element which is outside the scope of our methodical approach.

On the other hand, the act of formalizing the decision-making process can cause a disturbance in our system of values, because when our criteria are brought out into the open and weighed we may realize that they are inconsistent, and this may lead to some re-adjustment. An example which has been used several times in another context is the value of life. Some people believe that human life is priceless. Yet they will not agree with the spending of more than a certain amount of money in the building of better roads to make travel safer. If they were to work out the implications of the amount of money that they think should be spent on roads they might have to face up to a reassessment of the value which they put on human life.

For a long time the English educational system has made use of a formal test to divide children into two grades in order to decide which type of school they should go to. It is argued vociferously by some that this has distorted our value system and created a view that to be a 'grammar school' type of child is success and to be a 'secondary modern' type is failure.

In spite of its benefits, the law is a distorter of values. According to the law it is wrong for me to park my car outside my own house because there is a double yellow line there, but it is right for me to park it outside the home of my neighbour across the road where there is not a double yellow line. I have to do the opposite of what I would otherwise consider to be right in this matter.

Rules and regulations of all kinds have this distorting effect, so it is of the greatest importance to get our basic philosophies and policies worked out properly before we begin to make rules about the way we are going to make decisions. It is equally important to keep the system of rules flexible so that we can review it periodically and make adjustments to ensure that the outcomes of our decisions are what we really want them to be.

SUMMARY

The strategic way to approach decision-making is to begin by considering such general questions as the following.

1. Have the courses of action I am considering been constructed methodically? Are they capable of solving the problem? Have enough courses been considered?
2. How can I avoid carelessness in this decision?
3. Is this an urgent decision, where I need either to go all out for success or all out to avoid failure?
4. Is this a case for decisiveness?
5. Is this a case for taking plenty of time over the decision?
6. Am I making this decision in accordance with the values I believe in?

EXERCISES

1. The manager of a department store decides that all the sales staff should wear a uniform, in order to help them to identify themselves with their job. In what circumstances would this be a good decision and in what circumstances would it be a bad decision?

2. Sometimes a committee can be seen to be trying to reach agreement rather than to find the best solution to a problem. What might be the cause of this, and what should be done about it?

3. My boss calls me into his office and says, 'I believe you know Charlie Staircase. He has applied for a job here. Do you think we should take him on?' What should I say in reply?

4. John goes into an art shop and asks, as he often does, for a number 40 size tube of Titanium White oil paint. The assistant says, 'There is no such thing as a number 40 size tube, sir. Would you like a size 14?' How should John deal with this situation? What is the reason for your advice?

5. At their AGM the members of the Acton Tent and Bivouac Club are asked to vote in order to indicate whether they want to hold their next summer camp at Bacton or Clacton. What would be a rational reaction to this request, given that this is the first time they have heard about the matter?

6. A and B are running a race to a point on the far side of a wood. A is the faster runner and is just ahead of B. All of a sudden they come to a place where there is a choice of two ways. A takes the left turn. What should B do? Why?

7. You are desperately trying to contact Mr. D to let him know that a meeting that was to take place tomorrow has been cancelled. You make a telephone call to his home during the evening before the meeting and you find that you are speaking to a young child, who explains that 'Daddy has not come home yet'. What should you do? Why? Will your action solve the problem?

8. If someone says he wants to provide the best possible education for his children, what does he mean? How can he tell whether any particular form of education meets his requirements?

9. You are driving round a car park looking for a space and come to a sign which tells you to turn left. But just ahead a car drives out of a parking space and departs. Would you obey the sign or go on and park in the vacated space?

10. What is the value of a human life?

11. If you are asked by someone to help them to make a decision and they appear to have no clear objectives, what should you do?

12

Planning the Decision-making Procedure

STEPS IN DECISION-MAKING

The creation and development of courses of action should have been completed in previous stages, so in methodical decision-making we are normally no longer concerned about whether the courses of action are as good as can be. We are only concerned now with picking out the best of the available courses of action and obtaining commitment to one of them. How can this be done?

Ordinarily we just go on thinking or talking about the problem until we feel that we have made up our minds, but when the problem is important and there is time to exercise greater care we can be more deliberate. We can build steps into the decision-making process to make it more objective, more impartial, and more dependable. We can be more objective by choosing a criterion for identifying the preferred course of action and a supporting procedure for evaluating the alternatives against the criterion. We can make the process more impartial by deciding upon these matters at the earliest possible stage, so that we are committed to them before we can become biased by knowing how the results are going to come out. Dependability arises out of the skill and care that we employ in the process of decision-making.

This line of reasoning implies that the sequence of steps should be as follows:

1. Decide on a criterion for identifying the preferred course or courses of action, such as 'take the best value for money', for example.
2. Decide on an appropriate procedure for evaluating the available courses of action, which in this example would establish how much value for money each course of action would give.
3. Evaluate each course of action accordingly.
4. Identify the preferred course of action.
5. Resolve to carry out the chosen course of action.

It can be seen from this point of view that systematizing the decision-making process does not eliminate the need to make a mental decision, but transforms it from a choice between alternative courses of action to a choice between alternative procedures. We can be assured that this is a move in the right direction because decision-making procedures are few in number, and with experience we can quickly learn which procedures work best for us in given circumstances, whereas the range of courses of action that we may have to select from may be limitless.

EARLY PLANNING

The procedure for decision-making should be planned as far in advance as possible. In some problems it can be anticipated right from the start and may in some cases be mentioned specifically in the definition of the problem. If it is not, then the next opportunity should be taken, which is to give some thought to it in the course of the interpretation of the problem.

When the situation is complex and unfamiliar we may feel like putting off our consideration of the decision-making procedure, but this is normally not a good practice. As we noticed in relation to the use of principles, one can see examples of methodical and unmethodical approaches in government reports. A most commendable example is *The First Report of the Royal Commission on Environmental Pollution*, which met under the chairmanship of Sir Eric Ashby and reported in February 1971. The Commission made a point of bringing out very early in their thinking and in their report the criterion for choosing what to do about environmental pollution. They expressed this as follows:

The basic criterion for deciding how much to spend on abating pollution can be stated as follows. First, pollution should be reduced to the point where the costs of doing so are covered by the benefits from the reduction in pollution. This criterion is easy to state in these general terms but its application raises immense difficulties which are discussed in paragraphs 23–24.

Secondly, the choice that has to be made is not only between pollution in the aggregate and all other uses of resources; it is also between various kinds of pollution. And in making this choice one must not embark indiscriminately on some hastily devised crash programme to deal with emergencies, though specific local crises do occur from time to time as with the 'Torrey Canyon' disaster. What is needed is a careful prediction of the long-term ecological effects of various kinds of pollution, together with a sober analysis of their short-term impact. But there is no time to be lost in trying to determine priorities, since improvements in the environment take a long time to achieve. It has taken many years and millions of pounds to reduce smoke and sulphur dioxide in the air; it will require many years and millions of pounds to improve the standard of effluent which flows into some of our rivers. It must, however, be recognized that pollution is to an extent indivisible, in that it is unwise to try to deal with any one form in isolation. For example, it may be undesirable to solve a water problem and as a result put contaminated solids or sludges on the land, or to deal with solid waste or refuse by incineration and pollute the air. The possible side-effects of anti-pollution measures need careful study.

Thirdly, since relative costs enter into the choice between different forms of pollution abatement, this choice does not depend simply on which forms of pollution appear to be the most 'undesirable'. For example, the fact that—as is shown later in this report—most kinds of air pollution have been declining in Britain over the last decade, does not mean that it is not worthwhile trying to achieve further reductions in air pollution; for it might well be relatively cheap to do so. Conversely, some other form of pollution may be much more offensive, either now or in the longer run, but the costs of obtaining a given improvement may be so high that society would not be prepared to divert resources in order to obtain a substantial reduction in this particular form of pollution. In short, both sides of the cost and benefit calculations have to be taken into account.

The Royal Commission then stated how they intended to evaluate the various alternative courses of action which they were going to consider during their investigations.

The only justification for the alternative approach to decision-making, where the choice of criterion for identifying the preferred course of action is delayed until some courses of action have been devised and evaluated, is that it is sometimes impossible to predict the distinguishing marks of the available courses of action until they have been carefully examined. I was once asked to join a group of people who had the task of judging some wines and deciding which of them should be bought. This was a novel experience for all of us, but the leader of the group knew enough about wine to be able to draw up a short list of characteristics such as cost, bouquet and taste. He went so far as to produce an assessment form on which these characteristics were to be compared, but in spite of these preparations we found, apart from the question of cost which was just a factual matter, that none of us had had enough experience of wine-tasting to know what kind of description or measure to put under each of the given headings on the form. So it turned out that we were unable to agree upon a criterion for identifying the preferred wine until after we had done the tasting and made our rather amateurish assessment of each wine separately.

We have already come across one weakness of delaying the choice of decision-making procedure, namely the risk of bias or partiality. There is also the further disadvantage that if we eventually find that we cannot determine how to choose between one course of action and another we may have been wasting much of our creative effort, because in these circumstances one solution is effectively as good as another and anything beyond one satisfactory course of action is super-fluous. For example, if a committee cannot make up 'its mind' on some issue because the members are not agreed on the criterion for decision, there will be no point in proposing more and more alternatives.

DEFINITE AND INDEFINITE-NUMBER DECISIONS

When we are making a decision it can be one of two kinds. One is where a definite number of courses of action is to be chosen and the other is where an indefinite number of courses of action is to be chosen. An example of the first is where we are selecting one candidate to fill one vacancy and there are several applicants for the job. An example of the second is where we go into a fruit garden to pick any strawberries that happen to be ripe. Let us call the two kinds of situation 'a definite-number decision' and 'an indefinite-number decision', respectively. We have already said that the first step in making a decision should be to decide on a criterion, but this cannot be done properly without the preliminary step of determining whether a definite-number decision or an indefinite-number decision is required. This depends upon the quantity of resources available in comparison with the number of courses of action that we have to choose between. Normally we only make indefinite-number decisions when the number of available courses of action is small compared with the resources available for putting them into action.

DEFINITE-NUMBER DECISIONS

If a definite number of courses of action is to be selected, it needs to be made clear what counting procedure is to be used for allocating the courses of action to categories. In nearly every practical case, the counting procedure is based on a process of marshalling the courses of action into an order of preference or rank, so that the best one or the best six, top ten, etc., can be counted off. It is necessary to stipulate the quality or qualities to be assessed, the principle upon which the ordering or ranking is to be made, the number to be counted, and the rule for identifying the chosen course of action. In such statements as the following, this information is either given or implied.

1. 'We shall adopt the plan which gives us the greatest competitive advantage.'
2. 'Please give me an itinerary for the quickest route from Gloucester to Newcastle.'
3. 'We have only sufficient time to deal with the four most urgent items on the agenda.'
4. 'We are going to give a free dinner to every 100th customer of this restaurant.'

INDEFINITE-NUMBER DECISIONS

If an indefinite-number decision is required, we need to specify for each of the categories a critical standard which must be reached by a course of action in order to be allocated to it. This entails defining the qualities by which the different courses of action are to be evaluated and stating a level or degree of that quality which is to be associated with each category. For example, the police may set out to deter motorists from speeding, and therefore they may observe a stretch of roadway and stop and prosecute any motorists who exceed a certain speed. A farmer may wish to separate sheep which are undersized from the rest of the flock. He may therefore examine them all and judge by eye which are to be placed in the 'undersized' category.

QUALITIES AND CRITERIA OF PREFERENCE

The value of a decision depends upon the choice of qualities which we use as the basis of the criteria for assessing and comparing the alternative courses of action. No amount of method will enable us to make a good decision if it is based on the wrong qualities. So how can we select them, and how can we test whether or not we have selected them soundly?

There are several ways of collecting a list of qualities from which a selection may be made. If a methodical approach has been made to the problem from the outset, it will already have been ascertained that the courses of action being considered are all capable of solving the problem, and the principles that were followed in constructing them will show directly which qualities should be used in setting the criteria. But if the decision has to be made without this advantage, it will be necessary to go back to the beginning again and discover the real objective of the decision and hence what qualities should be considered.

Sometimes the objective is of such a nature as to point clearly towards the appropriate qualities. Here are some examples.

Suppose that somebody wishes to buy a new set of crockery for use at home. There is nothing in this objective to indicate what will be acceptable and what will not. But if this person breaks a cup or saucer and sets out to replace it, it is obvious that the replacement needs to match the rest of the set in shape, size, pattern and colour. In deciding whether to accept what is offered in the shops the person concerned may take a piece from the set along to the shop for comparison. The question of the exactness of the match is, however, another matter.

A friend is going to emigrate. Our objective is to give him a present that will remind him of the times we have spent together. This will be important in deciding what to buy him. Contrast this with the less specific objective of buying someone a birthday present. In this case there is nothing in the objective leading so clearly towards the decision-making procedure.

If the present objective is to select among candidates for a job, the nature of the job will be a fruitful source to analyse in order to identify the qualities required. Usually even wider objectives are known more or less explicitly, such as the general objectives of the organization in which the vacancy exists or the system of values which traditionally governs the way in which the organization works and chooses its people.

Further areas in which to seek for relevant qualities may be indicated by the circumstances of the problem. It might be important to know whether the candidates for a job are available immediately or whether they will have to give notice. A forthcoming reorganization might mean that the ability and willingness of a candidate to move his home in the near future would affect his suitability for appointment.

Naturally, there are many instances where the objective does not give a clear indication about the method by which the decision ought to be made. In these circumstances it is advisable to try to imagine how the decision will have to be made even though the decision-making stage has not yet been reached. This applies particularly in investigations where advice or other information will have to be gathered for the decision. It is usually a straightforward matter to identify various ways in which the information could come out, and then think about the way the decision would go in each of these instances. If we do not do so, we run the risk of wasting a considerable amount of the effort put into the collection of information, because we may collect information that we do not know how to deal with.

For example, suppose that an investigator is trying to decide what is a fair day's work for members of a certain group of people, so that work can be distributed more fairly among them in the future. He has no clear idea about this, but thinks it should be possible to ask all the people in the group for their opinions. Each one replies by saying that a fair day's work is what he does in an average day, and describes this in detail. The investigator has collected a great deal of data but is in no better position to make his decision than he was at the outset. If he had taken the trouble to imagine the sort of replies that his question would elicit and asked himself what he would do with the data he would have been able to foresee this result and might have looked for a better way to tackle the problem.

A similar method of identifying qualities for setting criteria is to consider the likely consequences of implementing the proposed course of action. This exercise shows up areas of potential advantage and disadvantage and is a useful preparation for the next stage of implementation.

Here are some useful questions to ask when trying to work out the consequences of a proposed course of action.

1. What could happen if this course of action is carried out—to what and to whom?
2. How likely is it to happen?
3. What would be the gains and losses in each case?

4. Is this a situation where there is predominantly a possibility of a large gain or a large loss?

Lastly, the ever-useful device of examining critical incidents, where things have gone wrong in the past, will yield information about significant qualities to consider for rejecting courses of action, and hence further indications of positive qualities to be preferred. For example, we might attach importance to the quality of colour-blindness in the selection of staff for a special job if we have found that it has been the cause of mistakes by previous employees, and therefore we might give all future candidates a test of colour vision.

SETTING CRITICAL STANDARDS—PITFALLS IN TRYING TO BE PRECISE

Although the mathematical and statistical content of this book is virtually nil, a number of the ideas that we are considering were thought out by mathematicians and statisticians and have been brought to our notice through their efforts. One of these concerns the difficulties that we always face when trying to set limits to some quality or quantity in order to come to a decision, Jerzy Neyman and E. S. Pearson being the statisticians concerned. They identified two ways in which it is possible to be wrong in judging against critical standards or limits. If we make the limits too narrow we may reject something that is really acceptable or make a distinction where there is no real difference. If we make the limits too wide we may accept something that we really ought to have rejected or fail to see a difference that is really there. It has since become common amongst statisticians to speak of these two situations as 'errors of the first and second kind'.

Here are some simple examples to illustrate the point. Suppose that admission to a school is decided by an entrance examination. If the pass mark is rather high there is a considerable risk of rejecting students who are really good enough —an error of the 'first kind'. But if the pass mark is set rather low there is a considerable risk of accepting students who are not really good enough—an error of the 'second kind'. Clearly, the limiting examination mark needs to be set at a level which will produce an acceptable compromise, a judicious balance between the two kinds of error. Similarly, if I want to buy a new suit of clothes I know that it would be unwise to be too inflexible about the texture, colour, and pattern of the cloth, because that could lead me to end up with no suit at all. On the other hand, it would be foolish to be totally indiscriminate about it because I might easily buy something that I would soon come to dislike. This sounds all rather obvious, but the situation we are discussing is a trap into which many people fall at one time or another. For an example of the 'first kind' we know that there are numbers of men and women who live solitary lives because they were so particular in choosing a partner in life that they never found anybody they wanted to get married to. The distress that has been caused through errors of the 'second kind' in the marriage problem is painfully obvious.

There are exceptional situations in which the dilemma does not occur, but these are uncommon and usually somewhat artificial. In a horse race, for example, we are happy to employ the most precise methods available for ascertaining the identity of the first, second, and third horses past the winning-post. A closer finish, in fact, makes a better race.

What can we do to avoid the pitfalls in setting limits and standards? It all depends on being able to get reliable information for predicting the effect that the setting of a limit or standard will have. If we have kept records of our routine decisions and their outcomes we may possess data which can be used for this purpose, but even if we have had no experience at all of a given situation we may still be able to get useful information about it by using a model or representation of some kind with which to simulate it. In business life many opportunities are missed because of a lack of appreciation of the advantages of exploring the unknown by trials and experiments, which can usually be made quickly and without much disturbance to ongoing activities. If the information is available we can work out or guess where a suitable compromise will lie, but if the information is not there then it is wise to keep our options open for as long as possible and delay the imposition of limits until further information is received. For example, during the fuel crisis of 1973, the British govern-

ment decided to make a precautionary issue of ration books
for petrol. The coupons in them were printed not in gallons
but in arbitrary units. This avoided the need to fix the ration
before it was known how much petrol would be available for
distribution during the period concerned. Too small a ration
would have caused unnecessary disruption and hardship, and
too large a ration would have meant that some people would
not be able to get their full ration.

EVALUATING THE COURSES OF ACTION

The evaluation of courses of action, like all the small steps
making up the larger stages of problem-solving, has to connect
up logically with both the step before it and the step to come
next. Once we have established the procedure by which the
decision is to be made, the evaluation must be conducted so
as to produce the information we require for the decision.

All we need to ensure, therefore, is that the evaluation meets
its purpose. If someone is interviewing candidates for a job,
all the time in the interview should be spent on gathering
information which will indicate whether each candidate is
suitable for the job or not. In the interviews which actually
happen in practice, it is amazing how much time is wasted by
the interviewer in talking. What he says does not contribute
to the making of a sound decision. The interviewer should ask
probing questions and it should be the candidate who does
most of the talking. It is true that the candidate also needs to
evaluate the employer, but even so, he should be given a
chance to ask questions rather than be subjected to a lecture.

The mistake is often made that evaluation is carried out on
qualities which are easy to assess rather than on qualities
which are pertinent to the decision. In the same example of
choosing among candidates for a job, it is usually the qualifications and previous experience which carry most weight
with prospective employers rather than the candidates' ability
to be leaders of men or their ability to deal with new situations
and problems.

One may buy sand from the builder's merchant by cubic
measure, but find that it is actually measured out by the
shovelful. Prosecutions have failed, and rightly so, when

motorists have been charged with having over a certain proportion of alcohol in their blood, whereas the measurement
taken was the proportion of alcohol in their urine. Usually,
the police are very methodical in the collection of information.
When I once reported to them that some cows had strayed
on to the road I was asked not what breed they were, but
what colour they were. Describing cows by colour is probably
a more reliable method than by breed, because in general
people are likely to make fewer mistakes in their identification
of colours than in their identification of breeds.

Another example, discovered by a 'profit improvement
programme (PIP) team' operating in the British Oxygen
Company was that the amount of LPG (liquid petroleum gas)
delivered to customers appeared to be less than that purchased
in bulk. The team found that some customers were served in
gallons and that this measure was then converted to weight
for invoicing. However, the conversion from volume to weight
necessarily involves the specific gravity of the liquid, which
varies from batch to batch and is also affected by temperature,
factors which were not being taken into account; some
customers were therefore getting more than they paid for.
An evaluation of the effects was made, sets of appropriate
conversion tables were produced to simplify the calculations,
and documentation was standardized. The result was a
contribution to profit of £2,000 per annum.

An instance of an unexpected form of evaluation came to
my attention recently when reading a book on fly-fishing for
salmon. According to the expert, the way to decide whether to
use a fly near the surface or a deeply sunk fly for salmon
fishing is to use a thermometer. It appears that salmon only
take a fly near the surface of the water when the air temperature is higher than the water temperature.

A common example of mistaken thinking in decision-
making is to be found in the application of ideas about the
motivation of industrial employees. Many decisions about the
way employees are to be paid and the working conditions they
should have are based on the importance of money to them or
the satisfactions which they find in various aspects of work.
What really should be considered first is what circumstances
enable employees to work at their best, and then it will be

easier to decide how they should be paid and otherwise provided for.

EVALUATING QUALITATIVELY

It may not be necessary to measure on a numerical scale to make the comparison we require. If the standard is a qualitative one, such as the ability to behave in an acceptable manner towards other people, it may be appropriate to apply it qualitatively by thinking and talking about it. Another example is the amount of russetting of an apple, which affects its grading for sale on the market and is easier to define by means of coloured pictures than numbers.

Numerical methods of measurement are only necessary when we need to make comparisons which cannot be made adequately by qualitative means. It is certainly not worthwhile to use numerical methods of assessment merely in order to acquire an appearance of accuracy. To do so may in fact distort the decision by giving too much emphasis to qualities which can be measured in numerical terms at the expense of ones which cannot.

A TEST OF THE ADEQUACY OF THE EVALUATION PROCEDURE

It is easy to be unaware of shortcomings in the way we evaluate proposals. If a woman sees in a television advertisement a beautiful girl with shining and gracefully swirling hair, who is extolling the virtues of a certain brand of shampoo, can she take this as evidence that the shampoo would make her beautiful and make her hair shine and swirl gracefully, and that she should therefore decide to buy it? Is it right for a father to buy a toy as a present for his child because he would like to play with the toy himself?

The only way to improve our skill at choosing the most appropriate methods of evaluation is to set a high standard of clear and logical thinking and get into a habit of critically analysing the decision-making processes with which we are concerned. Whenever we get a suspicion that the wrong criteria are being assessed, or that the method of evaluation does not fit the criteria, we should study the situation carefully by the process of analysis until we understand what is being done and how it compares to what ought to be done. We may ask ourselves the following type of question: 'If someone were to claim that this method of evaluation would provide evidence on which a sound decision could be made, would I accept it?' In a while this critical thinking process will become second nature, and will not impede the flow of work but actually speed it up and at the same time improve the quality of decisions.

FOLLOWING THE PROCEDURE AND RESOLVING TO CARRY OUT THE CHOSEN COURSE OF ACTION

When we have evaluated the courses of action it remains to apply the procedure that we had earlier agreed to use for identifying the chosen course of action. Remember that in decision-making we are seeking commitment to a course of action. For this reason it is best if we can make the decision by the means which we originally chose, although we must remain flexible and be prepared to learn to do this better as we gain new knowledge from our experiences.

The more serious and important the problem, the more careful we should be with the decision, and the more circumspect we should be. 'Sleep on it' is often a wise piece of advice to follow before committing oneself to a serious decision, especially if harm could come from a wrong choice. This is particularly true when we have made a decision under the influence of strong emotions. If we have written a letter in anger, for example, we may have solved the problem of expressing our feelings, but we may have done so at the risk of destroying a friendship or causing distress to the recipient.

Finally we commit ourselves to act. An effort of will is required here when we resolve to carry out what we have decided to be the best course of action. Some people call this step 'decision-taking'. If the decision is a hard one to take, perhaps because we anticipate that its implementation will be difficult, a review of the facts of the situation may bring encouragement. We have thought it out carefully and all our reasoning points towards a selected course of action, so this is what we must do. If we don't do it we shall not attain the objective and the benefits which can be expected to flow from it. If we really ought to be doing something else our decision would have been different, but the fact is that we have decided this way. We are going to test our decision in the world of reality.

TEST OF COMPLETION

The final test of whether the decision-making stage is or is not complete is to ask the following questions.

1. Have I now decided on a course of action to be carried out in order to solve this problem?
2. If so, what is it?
   Am I resolved now to carry out this course of action?

SUMMARY

Here is a recapitulation of the general procedure for decision-making which we have been advocating.

1. Decide on a criterion for identifying the preferred course of action. This step can be helped by ascertaining whether or not the decision to be made is a definite-number decision or an indefinite-number decision. A definite-number decision is made on the basis of a counting procedure for identifying the chosen courses of action and an indefinite-number decision is made on the basis of a critical standard which the courses of action must pass in order to be chosen.
2. Decide on an appropriate procedure for evaluating the available courses of action.
3. Evaluate each course of action accordingly.
4. Identify the preferred course of action.
5. Resolve to carry out the chosen course of action.

The ordinary way to make a decision is to go on thinking about the problem until we have made up our minds what to do. On the other hand, the methodical approach sets out to make decision-making more deliberate and objective by offering a definite and logical procedure and a range of important principles which may apply to any situation where a decision is required.

EXERCISES

1. If you were to buy a typewriter, would the choice be a definite-number decision or an indefinite-number decision?
2. Suppose that you are asked to recommend a good book to be read by a certain person whom you know well. How would you identify a suitable book?
3. Suppose you are asked to pick the best book out of six assorted books. How would you identify the best? How would you evaluate each book accordingly? Take any six books and apply the procedures you have specified. Were your procedures practicable?
4. You are the person responsible for public cleansing in a large city. You have to choose among several different proposed schemes for disposing of household waste, and these involve machinery for such processes as separation, composting, burning, grinding, etc. What criteria of preference would you adopt for making your decision?
5. In exercise 4 above, how would you evaluate the proposed schemes against the criteria you have suggested?
6. You are going to select some young people to be trained as hotel receptionists. What personal qualities would you look for in them, how would you set the standard which determines acceptance or rejection, and how would you measure the candidates against this standard?
7. Suppose you wanted to meet the tallest man in the world. How would you find him and identify him?
8. An insurance salesman is trying to sell you some insurance. How can you tell whether or not to accept his advice about the advantages and disadvantages to you of different forms of insurance?
9. You are a manufacturer of inexpensive gramophone records for selling by mail order. How would you decide on the amount of effort to be put into the inspection of records before they are sent out to customers? What would happen if the cost of inspection became too high? What would happen if the number of faulty records found

by inspection became too high? What would happen if the number of faults discovered by customers became too high?

10. You are at home and you hear a very loud noise like an aeroplane passing quickly overhead. A member of your family then comes into the room and says, 'Was that explosion in our house?' How would you decide what to do about this incident?

11. If I have a bad habit that is difficult to get rid of, how can I strengthen my will to stop it?

12. In problem-solving terms, what is the function of a jury? What is the function of a judge? What is the function of the law?

13

Techniques for Decision-making

COMBINING DIVERSE CRITERIA OF PREFERENCE

Whatever kind of decision we are making, there is a strong
possibility that we may have to consider a variety of qualities
or criteria of preference at the same time. If we are choosing
a package-deal holiday, for example, we may wish to take
into consideration the reputation of the firm, the type of
resort, the size of hotel, the location of the airport of departure,
the price, and several other aspects. The problem arises of
finding a way to combine our preferences for these qualities,
and we shall now discuss a few of the available methods.

SUBJECTIVE JUDGEMENT

Naturally, the first method to consider is our mental faculty
of judgement. The human brain is there to be used for this
very purpose, so let us use it whenever we can. It cannot work
without data, however, and we can easily overlook important
factors in a decision if we do not make them explicit. Therefore
it is wise to make a list of the factors that we wish to take into
account when making a decision, and think deliberately and
carefully about their relative importance.

NUMERICAL METHODS

Numbers can be brought into a decision-making procedure
for the purpose of combining criteria, and this is often useful

to get a decision made and accepted in circumstances where subjective assessments would not be acceptable, such as where people having many different objectives are in competition with each other. The numbers may help to bring objectivity into such a decision.

It can be useful to combine the numerical and subjective approaches by using one as a check on the other. If we assign numbers to the various criteria and sum them in some mathematical manner this can help us to find out whether our assessments of values are consistent with our subjective preferences.

COMMON CURRENCY—POINTS SYSTEMS

Nearly all formal methods for combining the values of different qualities are based on the idea of a common currency into which each quality can be converted. This can be arbitrary, as in a system of points, or it can be a specific means of exchange, such as money. In its simplest form, a system of points can be set up by constructing a list of advantages and awarding a point for each advantage possessed by each course of action. The disadvantages can either be counted separately, so that the comparison of the courses of action can be made firstly on the basis of advantages and secondly on dis-advantages, or else the disadvantages can be given a negative value and be combined arithmetically with the advantages.

WEIGHTED POINTS

Suppose that we are going to buy a motor-car. By specifying our general objective we can quickly produce a short list of cars which are worth considering. As this is a definite-number decision we need to have a counting procedure. In this instance it will be to take the first car from our short list which has the highest value of weighted points. We may choose to award points for, say, external appearance, internal comfort and convenience, engine performance, economy in running and maintenance, safety features, other equipment, and price. At the simplest level we can award one point to any car which possesses any one of these features to a suitable degree. Or, we can allocate points on a scale, say from 1 to 5.

The idea of weights is to adjust the values of the points in proportion to the relative values of the qualities for which they are awarded. Thus if we value safety features three times as much as other equipment, we should give a weighting factor three times as great. Only a small range of weights is usually necessary, such as from 1 to 3. We might arrive at a list of weights such as the following.

External appearance	2
Internal comfort and convenience	1
Engine performance	2
Economy in running and maintenance	1
Safety features	3
Other equipment	1
Price	2

Suppose we are considering four cars, the Dragon, the Deer, the Ox, and the Cheetah. Our assessment of points might be as follows, and the weights or weighting factors would then be applied as shown in Table 2.

From the totals of the weighted points it appears that the Ox has the best combination of factors and merits first place

TABLE 2.   Example of weighted points

Features	Weight	DRAGON		DEER		OX		CHEETAH	
		Points	Wt × Pt	Points	Wt × Pt	Points	Wt × Pt	Points	Wt × Pt
External appearance.	2	0	0	1	2	0	0	1	2
Internal comfort and convenience	1	0	0	0	0	1	1	1	1
Engine performance .	2	1	2	0	0	1	2	1	2
Economy	1	0	0	1	1	0	0	0	0
Safety features......	3	0	0	1	3	1	3	0	0
Other equipment....	1	1	1	0	0	1	1	1	1
Price..............	2	0	0	1	2	1	2	0	0
Total Wts × Pts.....			3		8		9		6

in order of preference. A more refined scheme of points could have been used, such as to allot points on a scale of 1 to 5 or any other number, but the outcome would probably not have differed very much. There is in fact a disadvantage in using long scales of points, because they make it difficult to avoid thinking about the relative values of the qualities whilst the points are being allocated, which means that there is a tendency for the weights to be used twice over.

Another word of warning is necessary when using criteria which are not independent of each other, or in other words which overlap in their meanings. In the example of buying a car it could well be that when we are assessing the internal comfort and convenience we are also thinking about safety and other equipment at the same time. If we add up the points we are again adding some aspects twice over and therefore some adjustment should be made. To work it out properly with overlapping criteria a much more complicated mathematical procedure is required, which is beyond the scope of this book.

OTHER METHODS

The literature of decision-making abounds in methods of refining the process of quantifying and comparing the values of different criteria. Anyone who wishes to study this subject further should have no difficulty in finding suitable books and articles. In order to help in relating the concepts used in this book with others to be found in the literature, it may be helpful to consider the following paragraphs, which are intended to explain some elementary ideas in decision-making theory.

FORMAL PROCEDURES

To be formal is to go a step further than to be merely methodical. If we decide to buy the cheapest, that is being methodical, but when we define what we mean by 'cheapest' then we are becoming formal about it. Although there are many ways of being formal in decision-making, we shall confine our attention to a few well established ones which should be sufficient for an introduction to the subject.

CONSTRAINTS

The term 'constraint' is used in some accounts of the decision-making process. Constraints are best regarded as part of the objectives, but they are of secondary importance in relation to the main or central objective. If the problem is to purchase a tape-recorder suitable for use in a school, subject to a limit on expenditure of a certain amount, this amount of money is a constraint on the solution to the problem. Constraints are often expressed as limits of time, space, money or manpower.

PRINCIPLES

In the sense in which they are used in this book, principles are general rules to be borne in mind during the course of the work of solving a problem. They are guides to direct one's thinking towards the kinds of solution which will be satisfactory and acceptable. When principles have been established in this manner, criteria of preference can be derived from them by expressing a preference for courses of action which best conform to the principles.

If we are planning to set up an organization, we may adopt the principle that lines of communication should be kept short, or that groups of people who are separated need help in co-ordinating their efforts. Other examples of the use of principles were given in Chapter 10 under the heading of 'Where to start building ideas'.

MAXIMIZING

This means to choose the course of action which maximizes some criterion of preference, e.g. buy the ripest apples in the shop.

MINIMIZING

This means to choose the course of action which minimizes a disadvantage or negative criterion, e.g. buy the machine which requires the least maintenance.

SATISFICING

H. Simon coined this term to refer to rules like 'accept any course of action which passes the critical standard'. For example, to accept any offer over £100 for the sale of a picture is a satisficing type of decision. Satisficing is particularly relevant to indefinite-number decisions.

MINIMAX

The minimax method of decision-making aims at choosing the course of action which minimizes the risk of making the greatest possible loss.

EXPECTATIONS

These are sometimes called expected utilities. When the outcome of a course of action is not known with certainty it is often possible to estimate the probabilities of the various possible outcomes. Probabilities are assessed on a continuous scale between 0 and 1, where 0 signifies no probability at all, a half signifies a 50–50 chance, and 1 signifies complete certainty. If we multiply the value of an outcome by the associated probability, we obtain a quantity called the expectation. Thus, if a salesman has a 60% chance of selling a product costing £1.00 to each customer he visits, then the expectation of his sales is 60p per visit. The expectation is equivalent to the mean value in the long run.

Expectations can be combined with the other methods. One can choose, for instance, the course of action which maximizes the expectation of gain or that which minimizes the expectation of loss.

TREE DIAGRAMS AND DECISION TREES

Elbert Hubbard said that life is just one damn thing after another. That is how it looks in retrospect, but when we look to the future the picture is not so simple. Its quality may indeed appear harsh and bleak for those whose circumstances are unfortunate, but the future is never fully predictable. There are many ways in which future events can occur, and there is always a possibility that something totally unexpected will turn up.

A tree diagram is a useful device for illustrating a problem in which we need to think about the uncertainties of the future. It is called a tree diagram because it divides into branches which correspond to the various possibilities which might come about. Suppose that I am concerned about my job. I have a contract of employment which lasts for three years. When that period is over I shall have the option of renewing my contract or taking another job elsewhere. A tree diagram would show this situation as in Figure 9. The fork in the tree represents the decision that I shall have to make.

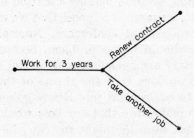

FIGURE 9.   A decision fork

However, if I do decide to take another job in three years' time, it might turn out to be satisfactory or it might turn out to be unsatisfactory. These possibilities can be shown as another fork in the tree. This time we are not illustrating a decision, but a chance event (*see* Figure 10).

Tree diagrams are made up of lines and forks and annotations to identify the alternative choices and the alternative

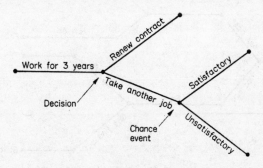

FIGURE 10.   A decision and a chance event

chance events. Extra lines can be inserted where necessary to enable various consequences and outcomes to be accounted for, or just to improve the clarity and balance of the diagram.

These diagrams are useful for the analysis of a problem and for explaining our interpretation of a problem to other people. But their full potential is only realized when they are annotated with numerical values, which make it possible to calculate the relative advantages of alternative courses of action. Tree diagrams used in this manner are commonly called decision trees.

Here is a simple decision-making situation which will serve as an introductory example. Suppose that we want very much to attend a professional conference. Normally, in such a situation there should be no problem, because we can just make the necessary arrangements and go. But in this instance it is not at all obvious that the theme of the conference is truly relevant to our present job. Before going, therefore, we really ought to make sure that our boss would approve. Yet if we were to ask him, he might say 'no', in which case we would not be able to go and would be deprived of a very pleasant and interesting experience. On the other hand, if we were to go without asking his permission and he found out afterwards and disapproved, then we would be in a most uncomfortable situation. Let us see what happens when we try to represent the various possibilities by a decision tree as in Figure 11.

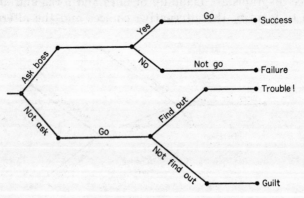

FIGURE 11. A decision tree

The first step in drawing a decision tree is to identify the decisions and chance events which will become the forks of the tree. The second step is to determine the sequence in which they are to be drawn. There is one decision in this example, which is whether to ask the boss or not. The chance events are whether he would say 'yes' or 'no', and whether he would find out or not if we went to the conference without telling him. The way we determine the sequence in which to draw the forks is to think of each fork in terms of action, and for a first draft set out the forks in chronological order according to when these actions will take place. The only sensible time to make the decision whether or not to ask for our boss's permission to go is before we go or don't go to the conference. This decision should therefore be the first fork to put in the diagram. After that the two chance events, concerning our boss's answer and his finding out, follow from the consequences of the first decision.

There are four branch endings to this particular tree, one for the contribution of each two-pronged fork in addition to the trunk-line of the tree with which we began.

We should not be confused by the fact that one of our chance events is the boss's decision to approve or not to approve our attendance at the conference. Although from his point of view it would be a decision, from our point of view we cannot anticipate with any certainty what he will decide, so until we have actually asked him we can only classify it as a chance event, which merely means an event which we cannot predict with certainty.

In some circumstances it is possible to express the value of the various consequences in monetary terms. When this is the case we can annotate the diagram with appropriate amounts of money. When money is to be received it is represented by a 'plus' amount, and when it is to be paid out it is represented as a 'minus' amount.

Let us take another example to illustrate this procedure. Suppose that an engineering firm is trying to complete the construction of a machine for delivery to a customer by a certain date. At present only one engineer is working on the project and there is a chance of one in ten that it will not be ready on time. There is a penalty clause in the contract which means that failure to deliver on time will cause the price to be reduced compulsorily by £1,500.

If a second engineer were to be put on the project as well, the labour costs would go up from £1,000 to £2,000, and the chance of not being ready on time would then become negligible. Would it be advantageous to engage a second engineer?

The decision tree diagram (Figure 12) illustrates the main features of the problem. The first fork illustrates the decision of choosing to employ one or two engineers. The second fork is a chance event which depends on whether the machine will be ready or not at the right time. The labour

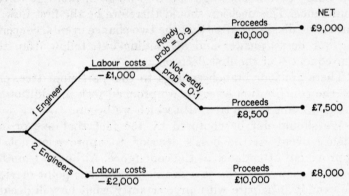

FIGURE 12. A quantified decision tree

costs are shown as £1,000 and £2,000, and the proceeds of the sale are either £10,000 or £8,500, according to whether the machine is ready on time or not, taking into account the penalty of £1,500 for failure to deliver on time. At the end of each branch there is a figure showing the net total cash flow found by adding all the items on each path, going from left to right all the way along the tree.

To arrive at figures for comparison in the decision, we calculate expectations by multiplying net total cash flows by the probabilities of going along the branches which lead to them. Thus £9,000 times 0·9 is £8,100, and £7,500 times 0·1 is £750. Adding both these products of the fork yields a total of £8,850, which is the expectation of the value of arriving at that fork and is the same thing as the expectation of deciding to employ only one engineer. We can now compare this with the expected outcome of employing two engineers, which is £8,000. In the long run, therefore, we would end up with more cash if we employed one engineer rather than two.

Decision trees are often sensitive to the values we put in to represent probabilities. As an exercise, readers may find it interesting to repeat the calculations using a range of values for the chances of the machine being ready and not ready respectively. Remember that these two probabilities must add up to one exactly.

Decision trees are widely used at the present time and can serve several useful purposes. One of my students used one to calculate a fair but profitable price to charge a customer for the use of a technical service, and then he was able to use the same diagram to demonstrate to the customer that he was being offered good value for money. My colleague Philip Montagnon uses decision trees to calculate the value of obtaining information which can help in making a decision, such as the advice of experts on the magnitude of certain probabilities.

SUMMARY

We have considered three ways in which techniques can aid the decison-making process, namely by combining diverse criteria together, by setting and applying criteria formally, and by modelling situations in which we need to anticipate events that may occur in the future. In all of these ways our abilities to make judgements can be disciplined and strengthened, as long as we use them wisely and remember that a decision made according to a set of rules will be subject to any faults or weaknesses that the rules may possess.

EXERCISES

1. Use numerical methods of combining criteria of preference in the following choices.
   (*a*) A present for a member of your family.
   (*b*) A televison or radio programme to watch.

    (*c*) A place to go for a holiday.

    (*d*) A new job for someone you know.

2. *John Jones's Problem.* John Jones, aged 35, lives at Alpham in a house of his own which is mortgaged. His wife is employed as a dentist's receptionist in Alpham and his only son Robert, aged 9, attends a local primary school. John's employers, The Modern Wallpaper Company, have offered John a job at their factory at Betham as a departmental manager, which is superior to his present job and the salary there is to be £500 per annum higher. If John takes up this offer, he will probably need to move his home to Betham and his wife will then have to give up her job. John himself will have to forego certain perks related to his present job, worth £150 per annum. If they move, they probably will take out a bigger mortgage and buy a larger house than their present one. However, it would be just possible for John to manage the journey to Betham daily, although this would cost more and reduce his leisure time at home.

If John were to let this opportunity go by, it is foreseeable that a new situation would then arise in exactly 3 years' time, when his boss is due to retire. There is a good chance that John would succeed to the post of Works Manager in that event and that would be a considerable step up for him. He would then earn £1,000 per annum more than at present and would have the use of a company car as well. This promotion would open up even further prospects of advancement for John later on in his career.

Before long, Robert's secondary education will have to be considered. If the Jones family remain at Alpham, then he will have a chance of taking the 11-plus test and if successful he will be able to go to a local Grammar School. However, if the family moved to Betham, this opportunity would not exist, and the Jones's would then be faced with the choice of sending Robert either to a comprehensive school or paying for his attendance at an independent school.

    (*a*) Draw a tree-diagram to illustrate this situation.

    (*b*) What is the first decision that John Jones now has to make?

(*c*) How far into the future will it be advisable for John to look when considering his decision?

(*d*) What are the significant features that should be considered by John in coming to a decision?

3. *The Calibration Problem.* A problem has arisen as a result of a promising idea put forward under the suggestion scheme of ABC Airways. One of their engineers has come up with a new idea for a device for calibrating a certain type of aircraft instrument featured in many modern aircraft including the company's present equipment. It is estimated that it would cost £12,000 to build the new type of calibration rig. Being an entirely new device, although working on sound mechanical principles, it is not certain whether the rig will be sufficiently accurate to obtain the approval of the Airworthiness Requirements Board (ARB) for it to be used in preference to the master calibrators used by the manufacturers of the aircraft instrument concerned. However, if the device should be successful, it would enable the company to carry out calibrations on its own premises and save the expense of sending them away to the instrument manufacturers who charge £30 per instrument. The average annual throughput is 500 instruments. If the device should turn out to be successful, the next thing to do would be to set up a line in the repair workshops for continuous operation. The cost of this work would be £5,000. Once the line is in operation the ARB would inspect the operation and decide whether or not to certificate the installation and allow the company to carry out its own calibrations. A further benefit that might possibly occur is that DEF Airlines might wish to make use of this facility, in which case ABC would sub-contract work from them and charge them £20 per instrument for an expected throughput of 250 per annum. To operate the line solely for their own use would cost £5,000 per annum in overheads and to undertake the additional work from DEF would add a further £2,000 per annum to the overheads.

Draw a decision-tree diagram to illustrate this situation. If, because of unfamiliarity, you do not understand all the information given, make your own assumptions.

On the basis of the position at the end of 4 years of operation of the proposed calibration line, analyse the factors involved in the problem and state what further information would be needed to come to a decision on whether or not to build the new type of calibration rig. Make suitable guesses to supply the missing information and try to come to a rational decision on the basis of your analysis of the problem.

4. *The Calibration Problem—The Plot Thickens.* During the consideration of the decision whether to build or not to build the new type of calibration rig, a fresh development has arisen.

The instrument manufacturers have heard about the proposals and have become interested. They have made an offer either to buy the patent rights now for £10,000 or to buy both the prototype calibration rig and patent rights as well for £40,000 if the ARB are prepared to certificate it. If the manufacturers obtain a successful rig by either of these means they guarantee to reduce their calibration charges to £25 per instrument.

Draw a decision tree to illustrate this situation and, making any necessary assumptions, attempt to reach a rational decision.

5. Consider a decision that you made badly, such as when you bought something that you did not find useful or when you took a job that was unsuitable, or when you chose any course of action that was unsuccessful. Try to determine whether you considered a sufficiently wide range of alternatives and whether you could have made the decision better if you had been more methodical. Were you handicapped by lack of time or lack of information?

6. Look through a newspaper and find an article which indicates a decision that someone has to make in politics, business, sport, etc. Imagine yourself in the position of the decision-maker and work out a method of making the decision by weighted points. If you are short of information where could you get it? In order to complete the exercise use your imagination and make suitable guesses to supply the missing information.

7. We make many of our decisions in groups, such as family

groups and work groups. Make a short list of examples of typical decisions made in these groups, such as where to go for a picnic or whether or not to buy a piece of equipment, and consider the best way to come to a group decision in each case.

Decisions affecting groups may be made autocratically or democratically. How does this affect the choice of decision-making method?

8. Make a list of six famous men and women. Put them in rank order of 'greatness', using your subjective judgement. Now work out a method of comparing them by weighted points, using several different personal qualities as the basis of your criteria. How does the result compare with your initial subjective ranking? What are the reasons for any differences between the two rankings?

Stage 5

IMPLEMENTATION

14

Preparing for Implementation

The stage of decision-making takes us as far as the point of committing ourselves to one or more courses of action. But that is not the final solution of the problem, because the fact that the course of action has received our commitment will not normally be sufficient to meet the objective. The course of action has to be implemented, which means that a further stage is required. This chapter and the next will deal with the planning, preparation, action, and control needed for successful implementation. During this stage the problem-solver stops being just a thinker and becomes also a doer. He has to take up the role of executive or manager. He has to manage the course of action that has been chosen, and this may entail a great deal of hard work. Sometimes the problem-solver hands the solution over to others to implement, but that does not really affect the principles involved. There are few special methods of implementation to learn. It is mostly a matter of doing things thoroughly and carefully.

PLANNING FOR IMPLEMENTATION—HOW MUCH PLANNING TO DO

In very simple problems the forethought and planning that has to be put into the evaluation of the possible courses of action on the way to making a decision is more-or-less sufficient preparation for implementation. Suppose, for example, that our problem is the one we have considered before where we have the objective of buying some clothes but we also have the obstacle that we do not know exactly what we are looking for. The decision on what to buy will be made after a little thought about why we need the clothes and what clothes we already possess. Then, once the decision has been made it will be a perfectly straightforward matter to carry it out. No further planning is likely to be required. We just go to the appropriate shops and ask for what we want. If they haven't got it we go somewhere else. However, if the problem is more complicated, there will be more planning to do. In buying a house, for example, a decision about the type of house is necessary, but because of the larger scale of the problem it is not appropriate or easy just to go out and buy one of the sort we want. We are likely to feel justified in making some kind of plan to follow in looking for a house so as to be more certain of satisfying the needs we have recognized.

The greater the importance of a problem or the more complex the course of action, the more necessary it is to plan the implementation with thoroughness and care. Or to put it the other way round, many important or complex ventures turn out to be less successful or more costly than was hoped because of inadequate planning and preparation before embarking on the chosen course of action. For example, in an interim statement published by the Laird Group Limited in September 1971, a loss estimated at £1,250,000 in their ship repairing company was announced. It was explained that 'The ship repairers loss is largely the outcome of the refit of the Ocean Monarch liner which is now virtually complete. It is due not to the effect of inflation on a fixed price contract but to a serious miscalculation of the amount of work involved in a refit of this magnitude.' It is unusual to see such a frank statement of an unfortunate business situation, but it shows how important it is for planning to be done with an amount of thoroughness and care in proportion to the scale of the project. It is also possible to go to the other extreme and use up too much time or effort in planning, which is at the very least a waste of resources or a waste of opportunities. If we spend too long in planning we may miss the moment when it is the ideal time to take action.

Between the two extremes of too little and too much planning lies the happy medium. How can we know how much planning is right? We need a rough guide to give some refinement to our guesswork.

It may be helpful to sketch out a graph to show an estimate of the financial implication of planning. Figure 13 shows a generalized hypothetical example. The horizontal axis repre-

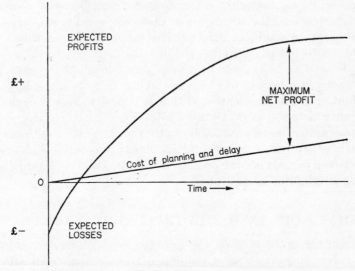

FIGURE 13. The effect of planning and its cost on profit

sents the passage of time and the vertical axis represents money. The curved line shows how the expectation (mean value in the long run) of the financial outcome of a project starts off as a heavy loss if no time has been spent on planning. Following some weeks of planning the break-even point comes, and after that the project is expected to become more and more profitable with more and more planning up to a maximum value. The straight and gradually sloping line represents the accumulated cost of planning and the cost of the corresponding delay to the project. Wherever the profit curve lies above the cost line there is a net profit, and the maximum net profit that can be made occurs shortly before the point where the curve finally levels off. If we could draw such a graph for every real situation we would always be able to make a sound decision about the optimal amount of planning required, but unfortunately we can never be sure about the probabilities of success and failure which are embodied in estimates of the expected gains and losses. For these we have to depend upon guesswork, supported by any relevant information that may be available about successes and failures in previous experience. It has been found by specialists in research and development that between 15 and 25 per cent of the total estimated development costs have to be spent on a project before it can safely be judged whether the venture is going to succeed or fail.

What this boils down to is simply that development work is a costly business in the long run and a risky business in the short run. The implication is that it is best to seek a flexible plan which will permit gradual development as reliable improvements become available, so that progress is evolutionary rather than revolutionary and one does not oscillate violently between periods of obsolescence of old ideas and upheaval due to the adoption of new ones.

WHAT GOES INTO THE IMPLEMENTATION PLAN

When the problem is on the grand scale, such as one which involves spending a large amount of money, implementation becomes difficult and complicated, involving many subsidiary problems that have to be solved along the way. In these circumstances a whole range of skills and techniques may be required, but we have no need to discuss them in detail here because the art and science of project management, under which title this subject is usually discussed nowadays, already has an ample literature of its own. For our purposes we shall assume that we are concerned with implementing a solution where the cost and complexity are considerable but not large, so it will be appropriate to suggest things to do which, although not applicable to very simple problems, may be useful in many others.

Basically, the technique of planning for implementation is

similar to that of planning for any other purpose, but there is a greater need for the plan to be comprehensive and thorough. Here is a check-list of items usually required for successful implementation. We shall discuss each one in turn, bearing in mind the assumption that the problem is of medium scale.

Planning and Preparation

1. Getting authority.
2. Getting financial and other resources.
3. Preparation of specifications and designs.
4. Programming of constructional work.
5. Selection and training of people concerned.
6. Determining who is accountable for what.

Action and Control

1. Giving instructions.
2. Supervision.
3. Monitoring progress.
4. Looking out for side-effects.
5. Recovering lost progress.
6. Dealing with contingencies.
7. Testing the new system.
8. Starting up the new system.
9. Operating the system.
10. Maintenance.
11. Review of objectives.

We can see from this survey of the activities concerned in 'implementation' that we have not really found the most appropriate word for our purpose. In fact we need to think of at least four different sorts of activity in this stage: the plans and preparations that have to be made to get ready to carry out the course of action, the course of action itself, and the activities that will have to take place to control the situation when it is being implemented. 'Implementation' is being used here as a convenient word to refer to all these activities, even though it sounds as though it meant just the 'doing' part of putting a solution into effect.

PLANNING AND PREPARATION

GETTING AUTHORITY

As John Donne pointed out to us many years ago, no man is an island, entire of itself. No man is self-sufficient and no man is insulated against interaction with other men. Whatever we do will have some effect on others. To think about such effects in advance when we are planning implementation is always beneficial. Sometimes it is just a matter of human fellow-feeling; sometimes an important question of goodwill. At other times it may be necessary as a matter of practical politics and sometimes it is essential because of a formal obligation to consult other people. In all of these circumstances we have a need to obtain authority, sanction, agreement, support, or sympathy for the course of action that we have decided to carry out, and to that extent these are closely related aspects of problem-solving.

This is an important matter, because without the authority of all concerned the implementation cannot be entirely successful, and without the authority of those who have real power the implementation may be prevented from taking place at all. The need for authority in this sense can be illustrated by reference again to the analogy of building a bridge. In trying to solve a problem we seek a solution which will fit existing circumstances and carry us over to the place where we want to go. But, no matter how much effort we put into the design and construction of the bridge itself, some work will have to be done to prepare the ground on which the bridge is to be built. The ground is an essential part of the system and will have to be depended upon to give solid support to the bridge during its construction and throughout its useful life. The people concerned in a problem are the foundations of the bridge, and without their support it will sooner or later collapse.

The essential point here is to be aware of the variety of kinds of authority that may have to be obtained in any given circumstances. The task of getting authority may prove to be a problem in itself, so we shall also consider some of the difficulties that may arise and discuss possible ways of over-coming them. However, let us not get confused here about our intentions. Although we are looking for ways of getting other people to co-operate, we do not need to be Machiavellian, and we do not need to get our own way at all costs. If other people find that they do not agree with our ideas and prefer not to join in, it is always possible that they could be right! We are as much concerned here with the art of avoiding dis-agreement through misunderstanding as with the art of persuasion. And, not wishing to get into deep waters, which can happen so easily when discussing human motivation, we shall restrict our attentions to a few practical points and avoid the more theoretical aspects.

GET THEIR INTEREST

Nobody will really be able to give our ideas full support unless we can get them to be interested in what we are trying to do. Obviously there are many ways of doing this. One way is to arouse their curiosity so that they want to know what we are up to. Here is an example from my own experience. I once asked Professor Alec Rodger for advice on this subject and have never forgotten how effectively it succeeded. I was at that time a new member of a photographic club and I wanted to persuade the officials of the club to let me try out a method that I had devised for judging photographs. Professor Rodger's advice to me was to draw up a form for judging according to my new method, then to sit down among the more influential members of the club at the next competition and start working away at it without saying anything, hoping to get them accustomed to the idea. I received this advice somewhat sceptically, but I carried it out to the best of my ability on the next possible occasion. The results were dramatic. My form-filling activities drew much more atten-tion than I could have hoped for, and before the evening was over, I was asked by the members to organize a full demonstration of the new method at the next competition meeting!

The principle of exciting curiosity can be adapted to a wide variety of situations, from enticing a cat out of a tree to enticing our boss to change his way of doing things. It all depends on devising a situation that will capture the other's interest.

GET THEM PERSONALLY INVOLVED

Most people like to feel that they are well in command of their circumstances and are able to make their own decisions. They do not like to feel that they have to submit to other people's will. They are much more likely to be prepared to commit themselves to a course of action which they themselves have planned or decided upon, than one planned or decided upon by others. This is why it is so valuable to arrange for all concerned to participate as much as possible in decision-making and problem-solving. Even when true participation has not been achieved it is often possible, by giving full information which they can use to their own advantage, to make others feel that they are to some extent committed to the decision that has been made. Once they have begun to derive some benefit from the results some people even start to act as though they were the ones who thought of the idea in the first place!

GET THEM TO WANT TO AGREE

It is a simple fact of life that other people will not automatically agree to give their support to our plans. The fact that we want them to co-operate is not sufficient to ensure that they do. How can we increase our powers of persuasion? This is a big subject, on which several books have been written. For example, Elmer Wheeler's book *How to Sell Yourself to Others,* is full of useful suggestions that can readily be applied.

Here are a few elementary suggestions from common experience which are always worth remembering when we need co-operation.

1. Explain our wishes to the other person gently, so as not to cause him surprise or anxiety.
2. Say 'please' and 'thank you'.

3. Demonstrate willingness to give as well as take. Friendliness and personal interest are welcomed by most people and are often more highly valued than a material gift.
4. Make the other person aware of what he will gain from the transaction himself.
5. If he has an objection, don't argue, but allow him to talk about it freely.
6. Be flexible, allowing the other person to have a say in the plan.

GETTING RESOURCES

The plan for implementing the chosen course of action cannot be carried out satisfactorily unless all the necessary resources are provided at the right time. This point is elementary and uncontroversial. Nevertheless it is one that has to be made, because it is far easier said than done. When implementation fails the cause can often be traced to lack of attention to the provision or use of resources.

It is useful to think in terms of the 'three Ms'—men, money, and materials—which are needed in any sizeable venture. We have to determine what is required in each category. In addition, there is the crucial resource of time; it is essential to provide enough time in which to carry out the plan properly.

Here are some questions that we may need to consider:

Men
— How many people will be needed in carrying out the plan?
— When will they be needed?
— What skills should they have?
— What knowledge should they have?
— What attitudes should they have?
— What training will they need?
— Will they be available?

Money
— How much will be needed?
— When will it be needed?
— Will it be available?
— What will be the further cost in interest, etc., in raising it?

Materials — What materials will be needed?
          — When will they be needed?
          — What qualities are needed?
          — What quantities?
          — What accommodation, etc., will be needed? Will this be available?

Any of these questions can turn out to be difficult problems when we try to answer them, depending upon the extent of our needs and the extent of the available supply. If there is difficulty, what we should do is to recognize the situation and tackle the problem of getting what is wanted, just like any other kind of problem. There are books on manpower planning, financial planning, project planning, and similar subjects which contain good advice on ways and means of dealing with these problems. And, of course, there are experts in these subjects who can give us advice or even do the whole job of procuring the resources on our behalf.

QUANTITIES

In the estimation of quantities it is hardly ever wise to risk erring on the low side, because it is very costly to have to buy in small quantities in order to make good a deficiency, yet that is the direction in which most of our inaccuracies of estimation lie. It is usually better to aim at a slight over-estimation because any remaining surplus can usually be put to profitable use elsewhere or disposed of without much loss. In the case of financial budgets, it is the maximum amount one is authorized to spend that one is trying to estimate and it is not wasteful to be prepared to leave some of it unspent, providing that some other venture is not thereby deprived of funds. On the other hand, under-estimating the expenditure required can lead to skimping, which creates a depressing situation for all concerned and makes real success almost impossible to achieve. If sufficient funds to do the job properly cannot be obtained it may be better not to try to implement the plan at all—in some circumstances the risk of failure may be a risk that we cannot afford to take.

SPECIFICATIONS AND DESIGNS

Specifications are detailed statements given to a designer describing the form which the solution to the problem must take. Designs are vehicles for communicating the solution of the problem from those who devise it to those who have to carry it out. Both need to be accurate and complete in order to make sure that what is done is the same as what was intended to be done.

When we are in a situation where we need to issue specifications or hand over the preparation of designs to other people it is essential that we should allow them to discuss the matter freely with us so that they can clear up any uncertainties about our intentions as quickly as possible.

If the designer cannot get a complete specification of what is required of him he should undertake to complete the specification himself and get agreement about it from the person he is working for. If he goes ahead working from an incomplete specification it is more than likely that the author of the specification will end up being dissatisfied, or the designer or supplier of the product will have to expend money or effort that he had not budgeted for in order to meet the real needs of the person to whom the product is to be supplied.

A number of objectives that may not have been considered before will become important and need attention in preparing the specification and design. These include simplicity of construction, adaptability, and the length of the working life of the product.

Unless we make a special point of it, specifications and designs are likely to overlook the vital human factor. Everything that we design to solve a problem will have to be suited in some manner to the needs and abilities of the people who are going to have to work with the product. Here we are getting on to the subject which is called ergonomics. Ergonomics is concerned with the following principal topics.

Characteristics of the human being

Physical abilities and characteristics such as body sizes, strengths, working postures; mental characteristics and abilities such as reacting, perceiving, decision-making, learning.

Man-machine relations

Displays, controls, information flow, automation.

Environmental conditions

Heating, lighting, noise, humidity, vibration, other factors affecting comfort.

Aspects of work

Fatigue, stress, errors and accidents, safety, pacing, endurance, work output, system effectiveness.

One cannot become an expert in ergonomics without years of study and experience, but to be able to see ordinary problems from the ergonomic point of view is not difficult and is not just the specialist's responsibility. A little thought about the suitability of the place where we work, the way the kitchen is laid out at home, or the way vehicles are designed in relation to the needs and abilities of their drivers, will give an indication of what it is about. For anyone who is interested in finding better ways of doing things or in improving the quality of human life, to read one or two books about ergonomics will provide a considerable amount of interest and many stimulating ideas.

It often happens that designers spend much time and effort in designing things that have been designed before. Even worse, as in the example in Chapter 4, they re-design things that are readily available on the market. This leads to much unnecessary expense, especially if the article in question is being mass-produced elsewhere and their design is for the production of small quantities. The way to avoid this is either to allow the designer the freedom to go and look for existing sources of supply himself, or else to support him with the services of others who specialize in knowing what is available on the market. This in turn depends upon being able to have trust and confidence in the designer. It must be demonstrated to him that he is responsible for economy as well as for design.

Designs are usually subject to several revisions. For this reason it is essential to make sure that all amendments to the design are communicated to those who are carrying the design out, so that they do not carry out an intention which has been superseded. It is also a good idea to arrange a final and unalterable dead-line, an agreed moment after which no modifications whatsoever are permissible. Unless this is done the chopping and changing that can take place may cause great confusion and the whole scheme may lose its momentum.

PROGRAMMING CONSTRUCTIONAL WORK

When there are a number of different activities to be organized there are usually various interactions by which the progress of one affects the progress of another, either to help or to hinder. It is therefore possible to prevent waste by arranging a programme which enables the different activities to be fitted as well as possible into the time available.

A simple bar-chart marked off in units of time, on which a line drawn to scale represents the duration of each activity is a useful device both for working out the best arrangement of the programme and for displaying the results. In very complicated plans the method of critical path analysis, which we shall not discuss here, can be used to show which activities are the most important to keep on time.

A very common mistake is to schedule the programme too tightly, by using the most optimistic estimates of the time required for each activity. It is more realistic to assume that there are bound to be delays and build appropriate reserves of time into the programme.

When the programme has been drawn up, we still have to ensure that all the resources are going to be ready when they are needed. This requires a good deal of foresight, and means that action must be taken well in advance.

The programme should be flexible, so that when difficulties arise on the way it will be possible to make fresh arrangements without disturbing the rest of the programme. If other people are involved it will be desirable to inform everybody concerned about the programme, so that they do not have to do their work just from moment to moment, from instruction to instruction, but are given a chance to anticipate what is going to happen and what may be required of them in the foreseeable future. This will enable them to understand more fully what we are collectively trying to do, it will give them greater confidence and satisfaction, and make them far less likely to make mistakes and omissions in their work.

SELECTION AND TRAINING

As the subject of getting the right people to do the job is so large, and so dependent upon the nature of the work to be done and the availability of suitable people, it is not a suitable topic for covering in detail in a book of this kind. The same applies to the subject of training the people who have been selected. A major part of the subjects of occupational psychology and personnel management are involved here. The reader who has much of this kind of work to do is advised to study it seriously by reading and by attending courses. All that we shall touch upon in this section will be of a general and strategical nature.

The objective in this part of the problem is to find people whose personal attributes are right for the job to be done. We can tackle this by analysing the task both from the positive point of view of the activities involved and from the negative point of view of the actions to be avoided. This gives us a picture or model of the requirements of the job which can then be translated into a mental picture or model of the kind of person who could do that kind of job. We can then compare the people available with this model person and make our selection accordingly.

When considering the abilities of people in large groups

there is a point which is frequently overlooked. There is a choice available between recruiting people of high ability, who are naturally scarce and expensive to employ, and recruiting people of lower ability who are less difficult to recruit and less expensive. Which should we go for? Depending on the nature of the task to be done, there will be one best decision in the long run. When it is a matter of recruiting for permanent employment it may be best to hire a mixture of people representative of all classes of the population from which the work force is drawn and arrange the distribution of work to make the best use of their various abilities. In this system there is no need to sustain a difference between the population of the firm and the external population, so that if people leave it is not difficult or costly to replace them.

Taking a wider view, there is in most companies an un-tapped surplus of talent which exists because of the inability of employers to use the talents of their employees to the full. Therefore there is always the possibility of locating under-utilized talent and putting it to use. It may require considerable ingenuity to discover and mobilize this, but there is much reward to be gained in doing so. One of the distinguishing marks of a really good manager is that he can create a situation in which his staff can realize their potentiality. This can be achieved by formally reorganizing the work so that it closely fits the capabilities of the people concerned, or else by giving the people concerned the responsibility and the freedom to re-structure their work for themselves, so that they do it in the way most suited to their capabilities. After all, in the long run it is the people who do the work who know more than anyone else how they can work best. It is only when they lack relevant experience and there is not enough time for them to acquire it that it is better for an experienced boss to dictate how the work is to be done.

When we come to the use of a formal process for selecting staff, as is usual for longer-term projects, there are several aspects in which simple methodical approaches are particularly rewarding. One of these is the classification of human characteristics, for which *The Seven-point Plan*, developed and published by the National Institute of Industrial Psychology has been widely used for many years. It is useful both for the description of jobs and for the description of people, and consists of a set of questions grouped under the following headings.

1. Physical make-up.
2. Attainments.
3. General intelligence.
4. Special aptitudes.
5. Interests.
6. Disposition.
7. Circumstances.

In the technique of interviewing, a planned and flexibly structured approach is especially valuable. The question of the use of stress in interviews is often raised. In normal circumstances it is highly undesirable to introduce a stressful situation into the interview. It is both harmful and un-necessary. The reason for rejecting this approach is twofold: firstly because the stresses that can be generated in a selection interview are not the same as those which one has to face up to in ordinary work, and therefore there is no reason why the candidate should behave the same way under normal stress. The other is that the purpose of the interview is to enable the candidate to supply to the interviewer as much valid informa-tion about himself as possible in the time available. This means that he has to be able to communicate at his best. Clearly he cannot do this if he is under stress. Interviews therefore should be conducted in such a way as to put the candidate at his ease.

The only notable exception to this is in the case of selection for technical work, where it is often necessary to probe deeply into the technical knowledge of the candidate. The way to do this was originally described in an article by N. A. B. Wilson in *Occupational Psychology* and can be done by any skilled interviewer even though he may not possess the same amount of technical knowledge that he seeks in the candidate. Apart from tact, it requires only the ability and determination to pursue a train of thought to its logical conclusion, in the direction of going into greater and greater detail on one or more specific issues. For example, I once interviewed an applicant for a post where an understanding of the functions of a mass-spectrometer was necessary. I asked the candidate to tell me the principle on which the mass-spectrometer works and he was quite unable to do this. On another occasion I was interviewing a man about a job concerned with the function of another spectrometer—an infra-red spectrometer. In this instance, the candidate was able to talk freely and in an enlightening manner about it. At one point I said 'I suppose that if you were to use the blackboard, you might be able to write a mathematical equation to illustrate what you have just been talking about'. Almost before I had finished speaking, he jumped up, grabbed a piece of chalk, and immediately wrote out a long mathematical expression and proceeded to explain with the greatest clarity and enthusiasm what each symbol in the equation meant and how it all related together. There was no doubt whatsoever about his competence in the theoretical aspects of his work. To ask a person to explain the technicalities of his subject can be a little stressful, but only if he is limited in his knowledge or his fluency of expression. This kind of stress can be quickly and definitely removed once the limit of the candidate's competence has been plumbed. The other kind of stress, caused by introducing a strong emotional element into the interview, creates a strained relationship between interviewer and candidate which is likely to persist for the rest of the time they are together.

DETERMINING WHO IS ACCOUNTABLE FOR WHAT

The traditional way to organize people is in a hierarchical order of subordination, with the chief at the top and various layers of officers and underlings beneath. Nowadays it is being realized in many places that there is an alternative to this by which various teams of people are made up to suit the occasion, the members being drawn from groups of specialists of varying kinds.

Whatever the principle upon which the organization of duties is to be based, the clearer and more logically this is worked out the better, and when it has been worked out it is desirable that the head of the group of people concerned should explain the role to be played by each member in the presence of the others, so that they know that it is his wish and his decision. It is very wrong to let out information on decisions of this kind only by private messages to individuals, leaving them to explain to their colleagues what they are supposed to do. It is unfair to those concerned and it tends to give the impression that the chief does not have much confidence in his lieutenants.

It is well known that it is not enough to give one's subordinates the responsibility for carrying out their duties. They must also be given sufficient authority to make it possible for them to succeed. This means that if we are in charge we should tell each subordinate what decisions he is entitled to make, and if this does not appear to add up to sufficient authority to carry out his full responsibilities, it must be agreed with him how the outstanding matters are to be dealt with.

SUMMARY

In this chapter we considered first the importance of thorough planning for implementation and the problem of how much planning to do. We then dealt in turn with the following topics relating to planning and preparation:

Getting authority
    Get their interest
    Get them personally involved
    Get them to want to agree
Getting resources
    Quantities
Specifications and designs
    Human factors—ergonomics
Programming constructional work
Selection and training
Determining who is accountable for what.

EXERCISES

1. Think of some changes you would like to make. How could you enlist the co-operation of other people concerned?

2. Make a plan to raise money for something you want, or for some charitable purpose. Decide what you are going to do about it.

3. If you have responsibility for the selection of staff, write down a statement of your policy on this matter and describe briefly the process that you intend to use for this purpose. Are your methods consistent with your objectives?

4. Take some small pieces of card and write a word or two on each to describe all the activities that you are responsible for or associated with at work. Put the cards together in small groups of closely related activities. Does this represent the way these matters are organized at present? If there are other people concerned, put their names on cards also. Use them to find the best possible way of allocating the activities to the people.

5. Try to recall an idea of yours which has not succeeded because it has failed to capture the interest of other people. Develop a plan for putting it into action in such a way as to cause no risk but to give those you wish to influence the chance to see what you are up to. Determine the most suitable time to put this plan into action and then go ahead and do it. If this cannot be done without the active co-operation of others, try introducing the idea to them with an unassuming phrase such as 'Would you mind if we tried a little experiment?'

6. The next time you realize that you need the co-operation of other people to accomplish your objectives, try bringing them into the activity of solving the problem immediately. Tell them what you are trying to do and ask them for advice on how to achieve it.

7. Other people will agree with us if they place the available courses of action in the same rank order of value as we do ourselves. Therefore we may need to supplement the value of some of our proposals in order to make them as

attractive to others as to us. This process is evident in any form of negotiation. Look in your newspaper for accounts of negotiations in political, commercial or industrial relations problems and identify the elements which have been added to supplement the basic value of the proposed courses of action.

8. Consider the place where you do your work. Are the surroundings there ergonomically correct? What can be done to improve them?

9. Are the people you work with fully trained to do their work? Are you? What further training would be desirable? How can you help to provide further training?

10. Some people always appear to be trying to influence the behaviour and conduct of others. Do you think this is because they are idealistic, or because they are inconsiderate or insensitive?

11. If you think that you ought to adopt some of the methods described in this and previous chapters, or that you should make any other changes as a result of reading this book, make a note of the points concerned and plan carefully how you will put these ideas into practice.

15

Action and Control

A sound way to think about the kind of instructions to be given to those who are to take part in the implementation of a course of action is to bear in mind two simple principles. One is that the people concerned will be in a state of mind which is different from our own. There will be certain things that they want to do already which may be quite different from what we intend. Therefore, we need to find out what their point of view is and take steps to bring them closer into line with our own way of thinking. The second is that we must communicate with them in such a way as to secure the results that we want. This means that our instructions must be capable of causing the right action to be taken and must not cause the wrong action to be taken. This may sound so obvious as to appear ridiculous, but the evidence of our common experience shows that in practice these principles are often neglected. The mistake that we so often make is to assume that the people to whom we give instructions are not really different people but are in effect extensions of ourselves who understand what we understand and do things the way we do things. Even in a simple instance such as asking somebody to buy something or to fetch something for us there is a considerable chance that we may give an insufficient explanation of what we are in need of or where it is to be found.

The process of giving instructions must also convey certain attitudes and the will to achieve the required results. Success in this depends upon the amount of agreement between our objectives and those of the person to whom the instructions are to be given. For this reason we should learn as much as we can about the other person's objectives and needs so that what we ask him to do can be adapted to meet his needs as well as ours. The instructions must not only be relevant to the other person's needs but also be seen by him to be so. If this correspondence of needs does not exist naturally, we may have to introduce an artificial incentive or reward in order to produce an equivalent effect.

In the actual imparting of the instructions it is the clarity of the message which counts above all other considerations. Anyone who puts his own self-importance first is unlikely to be good at giving clear instructions because he will be so concerned with being impressive that he will be unable to achieve the simplicity that is essential for clear communication. The words and phrases used in giving instructions should be familiar ones and the sequence of ideas should proceed gently from the known to the unknown. The pace should be controlled to give ample time for the message to be taken in.

If there are many details to be imparted, especially quantities expressed in figures, spoken instructions should be followed up in writing. Even in copying figures direct from one piece of paper to another a proportion of errors are bound to be made and for this reason all figure work needs to be checked two or three times to make sure that any errors that have crept in are eradicated.

Instructions should always be given direct to the person concerned rather than through a third party, otherwise the message is sure to become distorted. Although we have all had experience of this effect, we are unlikely to appreciate the extent of the distortion that may occur unless we set up a situation in which we can make a precise comparison of the original message and the final version that comes out at the other end. It is very easy to demonstrate this by writing down some simple instructions and then saying them to somebody, and then getting him to repeat the instructions to a third person and getting that person to write down what he understands of it.

In some circumstances it is impossible to communicate

directly with the people to whom one's instructions are to be given. The only way to prevent distortion as the message passes along is to insist that each recipient repeats the message to the person from whom he received it, as in the traditional ship-board routine, so that any distortions that take place can be corrected before the message is passed on.

The feeding-back of a message applies to the receipt of attitudes and feelings as well as factual information. In personal exchanges we have the opportunity to observe the facial expression of the person we are speaking to, his gestures, and the pose of his body, any of which can give clues to the way he is reacting to what we have to say. If we are observant and sensitive to these signs we can alter the tone of our message in a direction which will produce more of the kind of results we want, or we can try to find different words to express points which are evidently causing difficulty.

SUPERVISION

Wherever there is more work to be done than one person can do on his own, there arises a need for supervision. Supervision is overseeing. The role of the supervisor is to oversee the task which has been given to other people to make sure that it is done correctly and efficiently.

Correctness and efficiency are two different things. Either can be achieved without the other, since the correct results can be obtained inefficiently or the wrong results can be obtained efficiently. For example, if we send an assistant out to buy something he may get what is wanted but take all day over it. Or, he may come back very quickly having bought not quite the right thing.

The supervisor's first responsibility is for the correctness of the results produced by the people he supervises. The way to get things done correctly is no different from the way to solve any kind of problem correctly. A supervisor must be skilled in preparing and giving instructions, but even the best instructions cannot be relied upon as the sole means of producing good results. The further skills of control are required so that when things begin to go wrong corrections are made in good time.

The problem of getting things done efficiently is a little different. This is because efficiency is not a simple objective. Efficiency means using our resources of men, materials, and money with the minimum of waste, and the opportunities for waste or inefficiency are unlimited.

Skill in the efficiency aspect of supervision can be developed through careful analysis of the ways in which waste and inefficiency might enter the activities which are being supervised. Over a period of time experience will show which of the many potential sources of inefficiency are the most probable and important, and where preventive action is most needed.

It is possible to learn something from experience without making any special effort to do so, but we can learn more if we study what happens and keep suitable records. If we take the trouble to record and analyse the extent to which our resources are used, such as the way we spend our time, for example, and compare the results with what these resources are capable of, we shall get some idea of the degree of efficiency which we are achieving. We shall begin to understand the causes of inefficiency and see what kinds of improvement might be made.

For example, an immense amount of talent is wasted in businesses because supervisors have very little appreciation of the abilities of their subordinates and are not aware how productive they could be. Also, many sources of inefficiency are allowed to continue merely because nobody takes the time and trouble to find out their cause and see that it is put right. An example of this is the noise created by machinery, which could in many cases be reduced easily and cheaply but is commonly allowed to continue and cause difficulty in communication, discomfort, or even impairment of hearing.

A supervisor should therefore regard his role as the custodian of the correctness of what is done and the efficiency with which it is done. It is not his job to do the work he supervises but to overcome the obstacles which make it difficult for his subordinates to do their work correctly and efficiently. In this sense, therefore, the supervisor is not only the master of those under him but also their servant.

A supervisor should be accessible and approachable so that

problems which arise in carrying out the task can be brought
to him for attention. Otherwise they may be covered up and
remain unsolved or be tackled by subordinates who are not
adequately equipped to do so.

It should be made clear to all concerned which sorts of
problem are to be dealt with by the subordinates and which
should be brought to the supervisor. There is no easy way to
determine where to draw the line because it all depends on
the complexity of the task and the interests and abilities of
the people concerned. Only by studying the effects of different
ways of dividing up the task can the optimal way be discovered of deciding who does what.

The problems that people at work have to struggle with
are not easy to understand if the supervisor takes a limited
point of view. He needs to be able to see the situation from
their point of view as well as his own. He needs to know about
the kinds of obstacles that they regard as making life difficult
for them. Many of the problems that occupy a person's mind
at work are not seated in the work situation at all but are
brought to work from life at home.

For these reasons the supervisor should cultivate a sym-
pathetic outlook and get to know those who work under him
as well as possible, make efforts to find out what they need
and, within the bounds of economical management, provide
what is possible. It is usually found that the employee needs
a just reward for his efforts, respect, appreciation, information,
and understanding. He also needs to have a say in what is
done and how it is done, some variety in his work and a
general feeling that it is his job and not the employer's job.
The employee cannot provide for these needs himself, and
unless the supervisor is aware of them and able to see that
they are met some degree of frustration is bound to result,
which will lead to discontent and a loss of the will to do good
work.

The supervisor also needs to possess some of the characteristics of leadership. A leader is someone who is seen by all
concerned to know which way to go, to be determined to get
there, and to know exactly what to do about it. He sets an
example for others to follow. He ensures that everyone else
understands what is happening and receives sufficient help

and encouragement. He communicates by his presence and manner that action is necessary. Once it is clear that all is going well, he avoids interfering.

Although all great leaders have some desire for domination over other people, this is a strength which is more effective when held in reserve. It looks best when seen as an aspect of determination to do the right thing, and this may mean exerting influence on those below the leader or those beside him, or even those above.

MONITORING PROGRESS

In this life nothing ever works out exactly as planned. When a plan is to be implemented by a group of people it is impossible for them to be completely in agreement about what is to be done and they may not be capable of doing all that they set out to do. The materials and equipment with which we work are never perfect and the circumstances which affect the outcomes of our efforts are always fluctuating.

In this unstable situation all we can be sure of is that the results of the activities we set in train will tend to depart from the objectives we have set. We shall have to maintain a watch on what is happening in order to detect these departures quickly and be able to correct them before they become serious. This means that the plan for implementation must include the provision of time and other resources for monitoring progress.

Some thought needs to be given to the frequency of the observations and measurements to be made in the process of monitoring. This should be adjusted according to the value attached to keeping up with the programme. For example, if it is absolutely essential to get the project finished by a certain date, such as a building which must be completed at least a week before the date of delivery of some equipment to be housed in it, then a daily review of progress may be necessary because we cannot afford to be more than a few days out. In a situation like this it would be foolish not to include in the programme an allowance of time for contingencies, because once time has been lost it is usually very expensive to catch up again and sometimes it is impossible to catch up at all.

When there is no deadline for completion a weekly or monthly review of progress may be sufficient.

The frequency of measurements to be taken for assessing progress should be related also to the rate at which unwanted changes are likely to take place. For example, when driving slowly in a car with good steering it is not necessary to observe and correct its distance from the side of the road frequently, but when driving at high speed it is necessary to do this almost continuously. And if the steering mechanism of the car becomes worn and slack, frequent observations and corrections become necessary even at low speeds. Similarly, a project which is going steadily with few events happening on the way may need little monitoring. but a project with many complications and many opportunities for things to go wrong will need more monitoring, and a project being undertaken by an unskilled or unreliable team will need close and frequent monitoring. In discussing decision-making we referred to the mistake of making measurements too precisely. Similar faults occur in implementation. In book-keeping, for example, the tradition of making everything balance out to the nearest penny has been hard to overcome, even in businesses where errors occur of the order of tens and hundreds of pounds. In aviation the choice and design of instruments in the cockpit of an aeroplane is still strongly influenced by the wishes of test pilots and engine manufacturers who seek a degree of precision which far exceeds that required by the airline captains and their co-pilots.

As a rule of thumb, it is safe and economical to measure in units of about a tenth of the maximum amount of change that can occur between observations. Thus, it would be wasteful to measure the progress of building a brick wall by counting every brick that has been laid. The number of completed courses of bricks or the number of square metres of wall would be a more appropriate measure. Similarly, the degree of accuracy expected in the stock records kept by storekeepers is usually far higher than is really necessary. It does not matter whether or not all issues from stock are precisely accounted for. What matters is that one does not run out of important items and that one does not hold excessive stocks of expensive goods.

STATISTICAL QUALITY CONTROL

The statistical procedure of quality control is based on the idea of a standard to which the quality of output is expected to conform, and takes account also of the inevitable variations of quality which take place. Instead of setting just one limiting standard, bands of quality are defined, which distinguish normal variation about the average from the excessive variations which arise when some aspect of the process has gone out of control.

For example, supposing that a machine has been set up to make synthetic boards of a certain thickness and weight. It will be possible by statistical means to specify an average weight for boards and limiting weights above and below the average which not more than one per cent or some other chosen proportion of boards should exceed. Then sample boards chosen at regular intervals during production can be weighed to test whether the weight of the boards is tending to move away from the average value towards either the heavier or the lighter extreme. It will be possible to distinguish between a persistent change of quality and the chance fluctuations which take place in the normal course of events.

However, having discovered a trend in the quality of output, we still have to decide whether or not to do something about it. It is important here to be able to recognize natural oscillations and rhythms which will correct themselves if left alone. Aeroplanes and ships, for example, have natural slow swings to and fro in their movement which it is not necessary for the pilot or helmsman to correct. Similarly, human beings have a natural rhythm in their rate of working which rises and falls characteristically at different times of day. This does not necessarily mean that they are increasing or decreasing in skill or in diligence, it is merely a reflection of periodic changes taking place in the physiological systems of the body. When we are trying to manage any kind of system, therefore, we need to know whether such natural periodic fluctuations exist so that we do not waste time or energy in trying to adjust matters which if left alone would sooner or later return to normal.

LOOKING OUT FOR SIDE-EFFECTS

Even though the solution being implemented may be a good one, we know that not all of the consequences of implementing it will necessarily be good. Bad consequences can happen either because the objective gained is incompatible with other objectives that we possess, or because the action taken has unexpected effects on circumstances which were not regarded as part of the problem. Examples in the first category are easy to detect, in fact they usually become painfully obvious. Suppose, for example, that a manufacturer alters his product in order to be able to make it more cheaply. If the altered product is not liked by his customers, he will find out about it in a very certain manner when sales begin to fall off. Examples in the second category are more difficult to detect, yet they may be just as serious—perhaps more serious for other people than for ourselves. Because these side-effects are insidious a special vigilance is called for to detect and identify them.

Pollution of the environment is a class of side-effect which has only recently come to be taken seriously. Related to it is ecological damage in the shape of the destruction of the habitat and means of survival of various forms of life. Any industrial activity may be a potential hazard to the environment or to living creatures.

Within the industrial community a beneficial change in one place may cause harm in another. A thriving and successful port can attract trade from other ports that are not doing so well and thereby cause dockworkers elsewhere to lose their livelihoods. Within a single company to bring in a new technology may make more work for some employees and less for others. Providing new uniforms for one group of workers may cause jealousy and irritation among others. A new and improved method in a factory may cause older workers hardship because of the difficulty they may have in adapting themselves to it, or a new method of allocating work may be more efficient but may break up groups of people who are used to working together and thereby take away their main source of satisfaction.

The possibilities of unfortunate side-effects occurring are so many and subtle that we cannot expect to be able to foresee and to prevent all of them. What we are unable to avoid by preventive methods must be discovered and remedied. It is always wise to monitor the situation for which we are responsible and the environment of that situation during the period in which the new solution is introduced and for some time afterwards, looking for signs of trouble that may have been caused by the changes we have made.

RECOVERING LOST PROGRESS

In problem-solving terms it is a very serious matter when the implementation of a course of action gets behind schedule or escalates in costs, because these changes can nullify all the good work that went into the making of the decision whereby the course of action was selected.

When it is essential to complete a project on time and progress has been slower than expected, it is usually necessary to take emergency action both to make up the lost time and to increase the rate of progress. The only exception to this is when a large margin of time has been allowed in setting the date for completion. The key factor in success here is the speed with which the system is able to react when it is found that progress is lagging behind, because the sooner remedial action begins the less action is required—a stitch in time saves nine.

To recover lost time and to achieve also a better rate of progress is a costly business. It means that reserves of money and other resources must be available and standing ready to boost the ongoing work and propel the project forward. Some important human resources are also required—resources of co-operation and morale, to enable the people concerned to adapt to a faster rate of progress, to exert greater efforts, to adopt new methods, and set up new standards. Good communications are also necessary so that the changes to be made are quickly understood and the reasons for them are appreciated.

DEALING WITH CONTINGENCIES

Nearly every plan for implementation will run into difficulties sooner or later when some obstacle unexpectedly arises in the way. This is bound to happen because it is impossible to foresee every eventuality and it is uneconomic to take more than a certain number of precautions.

Contingencies are new problems which we have to face up to in the task of carrying out the plan. They need to be tackled in the same way as any other problem and the whole sequence of problem-solving stages will have to be followed. In one respect, however, there is a considerable difference between a contingency problem and an ordinary problem because solving a contingency problem may affect the chances of success or failure of a very important venture.

For example, it may be very costly to manufacture spare parts in small quantities but much cheaper to buy them. Nevertheless, if during the construction of an important project progress is halted because of a shortage of spare parts, then there may be a considerable financial advantage in manufacturing the needed parts. If purchased supplies have to be waited for, this will cause a delay in the completion of the project and a loss of the benefits that would have accrued from it during the period.

Strangely enough, an error is frequently made by doing the opposite, when a contingency arises in an activity of little value and is allowed to draw resources away from some other activity of much greater value. For example, the Managing Director may be held up by a telephone call on a relatively trivial matter whilst on his way to a meeting of senior managers. This will delay a considerable number of people in getting on with important work. A sound appreciation of the value of resources, especially the resource of time, is an asset to anyone who carries managerial responsibilities.

In the long term the way to reduce the harmful effects of contingencies is by learning as much as possible from experience. This means that we need to be able to recognize different classes of contingency, such as the following, and act accordingly.

1. Idiosyncrasies—minor aberrations of the system which may have to be tolerated.
2. Singularities—which are unlikely to happen again.
3. Unsuspected faults—which require corrective modifications.
4. Fundamental weaknesses—which may involve going 'back to the drawing-board'.

TESTING THE NEW SYSTEM

There are several good reasons for subjecting a new system to a series of tests before it is put into operation. Firstly, it is desirable to find out if the system will do what it was intended to do in order to know whether or not to go ahead. Secondly, there may be safety questions to consider and therefore it may be necessary to find out the limits of safe operation. Thirdly, there is the question of working out the best methods of operation, which it may have been impossible to be sure about until the system was built and made ready. Fourthly, in some complicated systems such as those employing computers for example, it is desirable to explore the possibility of causing faults by incorrect operation. If it is possible to make a mistake in operating the system someone is bound to do so in the course of time, but the consequences of this happening when the system is in full use may be so serious as to be unacceptable.

This is a very interesting and crucial stage giving many opportunities for the exercise of methodical problem-solving. The work of devising the tests may require considerable ingenuity and the carrying out of the tests is likely to call for patience and perseverance. The interpretation of test results requires logical thinking and sound judgement.

STARTING UP THE NEW SYSTEM

Starting up a new system is similar in many respects to the beginning of the work that was necessary for constructing the system. There is work to be organized and to be allocated to the people who are to operate it. These matters are seldom given enough attention and consequently many new projects run into difficulties. The starting-up phase is a period of great change for everybody and a unique opportunity for learning. Plenty of time should be allowed for adjustments and every chance should be taken to help anyone who is in difficulties to adapt to the new circumstances.

In the excitement of a new venture there will inevitably be a spate of mistakes and mishaps. But it should not be difficult to create an optimistic and supportive atmosphere and minimize the spread of emotional stress. The more serious consequences and failures in operating a new system can be reduced if it is possible to provide 'double-running' in which the old system or a reserve system is operated in parallel with the new until the initial running-in period is over. This may be costly but it is usually an essential safeguard. The only trouble that sometimes arises is that a great reluctance can develop towards the sloughing off of the old or reserve system, which can lead to the cost and complication of continuing to run two systems instead of one.

In the early period of operation it is essential to be on the look-out for snags so that serious troubles are prevented from developing. It is wise to keep a log of faults, changes, adjustments, repairs, and modifications. This will provide useful information for preventive maintenance and for the planning of future improvements.

No attempt should be made to exceed the performance limits that have been laid down. Any new system needs to be run in carefully like a new motor-car. A steady pace to begin with will allow everything to settle down to its proper function with the minimum of friction.

OPERATING THE SYSTEM

When the system is in operation we enter a new phase. Its nature depends somewhat on the duration of the expected active life of the system. If it is relatively short like an astronaut's journey to and from the moon, it will be a brief adventure, but if it is long like the life of a factory, it will be an extended series of events involving many repetitions of similar activities. In the former case one basic plan will be sufficient to cover most eventualities. In the latter there will be a need for many plans, one to follow another as circumstances change, and there will be a recurring need to replenish used-up resources and to carry out maintenance and repairs. In other words, a project which is extended in time requires the exercise of continued management and administration.

What can one usefully say about this in a few words? What is the essence of this type of situation in regard to the need for method? At least we can recognize that this is another typical example of a control problem, where the guiding principle is to set attainable standards and make sure that they are met, for this is the recipe for success.

In both the brief and the extended types of project there is work to be done, and effectiveness in work depends very much on the choice of methods and tools. In an extended project there is time and opportunity for improvement. If the desire to improve can be generated and there is a willingness to develop and try out new ideas, the improvements will come. These will bring increased success in the long run and ensure that the whole system continues to be lively and vigorous. In addition to deliberate improvements there will also be the need to respond to changes in the environment, which demands alertness and sensitivity to the outside world and the ability to make adaptive internal changes.

We are also concerned here with the problem of survival. Survival depends upon being aware of the essential requirements for continued existence and on making sure that their supply is not allowed to fail. Secondly, it depends upon being aware of the sources of danger and on setting up adequate defences against them. These are strategic tasks which should be given priority over any temporary crisis which may occur in the course of operation, no matter how alarming it may appear. In a supportive environment we can afford to relax a little, but in a hostile environment disaster will rapidly overtake us if we are unwary. For example, if we are operating a business in our own country we can safely assume a considerable amount of freedom from government interference, but if we are operating a business in one of the developing countries we need to be kept well informed of the intentions of that country's politicians, and to keep on good terms with them in order to avoid such risks as to lose our assets through a sudden decision on their part to nationalize our business and its operations.

MAINTENANCE

In designing any system that is to last for a considerable period of time some thought should be given to the question of maintenance. Nothing is permanent. Every material thing is liable to wear out, to get used up, or to deteriorate in some manner. The people concerned with the operation of the system are also not permanent because they may become ill or they may quit. Even if they stay with the system they may forget some of what they have learned to do. Every one of these changes will eventually cause a change in the performance of the system, usually for the worse. The problem of maintenance is the problem of maintaining the performance of the system in the face of these obstacles.

There are several different strategies to choose from for solving this problem, and we shall look at them briefly but in sufficient detail to give an indication of the circumstances in which they are appropriate.

PREVENTION

Preventive maintenance follows the policy of keeping the condition and performance of the parts of the system up to a certain standard. It has its drawbacks and its advantages. It can be wasteful if it is applied to parts of the system that would not fail even in the absence of preventive treatment. It can also actually cause faults to occur when it interferes with parts of the system that would otherwise be left alone. But it can stop the more serious types of fault from occurring by ensuring that the parts of the system are kept in good order. In some instances, especially where labour costs are high, it can save money. The cost of a well-planned round of visits to do maintenance work can be less than the cost of a number of special visits required to undertake repairs or replacements. For example, it is sometimes cheaper to replace items like electric light bulbs at scheduled times rather than to wait until they burn out and replace them individually.

CORRECTION

Corrective maintenance follows the policy of putting things right when they go wrong. It sub-divides into the vigilant kind and the reactive kind. The vigilant kind is where we actively maintain surveillance over all parts of the system giving more attention to the more risky and dangerous areas, and looking for signs of trouble so that corrections can be made as quickly as possible. The work of the coastguard and the forest ranger are examples in this category. It means that someone has to devote his time to active watch-keeping or inspection, both of which are tedious and difficult to do efficiently. The rarer the occasion on which faults arise, the more likely is it that they will not be spotted when they actually occur.

Corrective maintenance of the reactive kind is where we just carry on as usual until something goes wrong and then diagnose the fault and try to put it right. This is a policy which does not require any planning at all, but if it is appropriate to the situation it can be highly efficient. It is risky because it means doing nothing except when something has already gone wrong. Consequently it is only appropriate when nothing very serious will happen if things do go wrong. The policy of 'management by exception' comes into this category.

PLANNED OBSOLESCENCE

A policy which has the advantage of reducing the need for expensive replacements is to design the system so that it can be expected to continue to function adequately for most of the period when it is needed and deteriorate or wear out when it has finished serving its purpose.

The components of modern motor-cars appear to be designed according to this policy so that they all tend to wear out at more or less the same time, although regular routine maintenance is assumed to take place as well during the life of the car.

REPLACE RATHER THAN REPAIR

When the cost of repair is as high as the cost of replacing a faulty part it is often simpler to throw the old one away and fit a new one. This policy is expedient, and the replacement can usually be carried out by people whose skills are less than those required for repair work. However, at a time when the world is rapidly using up its valuable resources of raw materials by converting them into junk we should think very carefully about every decision of this kind. Already such recent innovations as the non-returnable bottle are being criticized as a step in the wrong direction. We have here to weigh the value of our business objectives against the value of conserving natural resources.

A WELL-BALANCED MAINTENANCE POLICY

In the larger and more complex systems a mixture of maintenance policies may be advisable in order to get the best overall results. A well-balanced scheme of maintenance will take account of the way the various parts of a system are likely to deteriorate, the seriousness of the type of failure liable to occur, and the relative costs of repair and replacement. In practice we attain a fairly well-balanced scheme after a period of learning by our mistakes, but usually we end up with a scheme which tends to give too much attention to the more trivial parts of the system and not quite enough to the more vital parts. Perhaps the most effective way of improving the efficiency of maintenance in general would be to adopt a policy of concentration of effort, whereby when something goes wrong as many resources as can effectively be applied are brought to bear on the fault to rectify it as quickly as possible. This applies particularly to the maintenance of roads and other essential services, both public and private.

A less dramatic but no less important area needing attention is the system of communications for arranging corrective maintenance work. The obstacle here is the allocation of responsibility. Is it the user of the system who is responsible for its maintenance, or is it the maintenance man? It is essential to get this agreed and understood for otherwise many faults that occur will not receive attention; the user will say 'It's no use reporting a fault because nobody ever comes to put it right' and the maintenance man will say 'Nobody ever tells me when there is a fault, so how can I be expected to repair it?' The prime responsibility of the user is to produce the output required from the system. So when there is a fault which affects or may affect output he should try to get it repaired quickly. The responsibility of the maintenance man is to keep the system serviceable for as much as possible of the period of time when it is needed. He should therefore develop a working relationship with the user and expect to be kept informed about the state of the system from a user's point of view. A mutual trust is required for this which can only be sustained if the passing of information is matched by a willingness to listen and to respond.

The efficiency of the maintenance scheme is partly pre-determined in the specification and design of the system. The system can be designed with a large safety factor so that it is unlikely for any serious fault to develop in its lifetime and less maintenance is needed. Or the system can be designed on the assumption that deterioration will occur, that equipment should be easily accessible for maintenance, and that maintenance work should not cause the deterioration of parts such as fastenings and connections. In very advanced types of system a considerable amount of maintenance can be made automatic.

REVIEW OF OBJECTIVES

After the new system has settled in and has begun to perform steadily, the time will come to assess the overall achievements and to consider whether or not the system is enabling us to reach the objectives for which it was created. Apart from the information this comparison gives us about needs for improving the system, it will provide an opportunity to assess our judgement and our general ability to devise and decide upon sound courses of action and implement them effectively.

But the world is not static. Events are marching on all the time. The circumstances in which we work and go about our business will eventually become quite different from what they are now, and our own needs and values will alter as time passes. These changes will affect the validity of our objectives, which could become outdated if we did not take care to revise them periodically. There is a vital need to review our objectives from time to time and to reconsider whether the ones we are using to govern our operations are still appropriate. 'Vital' is the correct word here because the choice of objectives can be a matter of life and death, either for a business or an individual person. In recent times several large and highly regarded businesses have accidentally destroyed themselves by pursuing objectives beyond their capabilities, not realizing that they had insufficient financial or technical strength. On the other hand, many other businesses, by modernizing their objectives and making them compatible with current market conditions, have revitalized themselves, rising out of a state of weakness and decay into a new period of growth. So it has been also with individual men and women, some of whom have damaged their lives and happiness by over-rigid adherence to inappropriate personal objectives, whereas others have found contentment or perhaps new inspiration by throwing away old objectives which were unattainable and taking up more realistic ones better matched to their abilities and circumstances.

SUMMARY

The second part of implementation is the executive part, where the course of action really becomes action. The list of topics covered in this chapter includes the steps required to get the action going and the steps we can take to control the outcome.

Giving instructions
Supervision
Monitoring progress
    Statistical quality control
Looking out for side-effects
Recovering lost progress
Dealing with contingencies

Testing the new system
Starting up the new system
Operating the system
Maintenance
 Prevention
 Correction
 Planned obsolescence
 Replace rather than repair
 A well-balanced maintenance policy
Review of objectives.

The final review of objectives completes the cycle and enables us to evaluate the whole activity of trying to solve the problem and to learn as much as possible from our experiences.

EXERCISES

1. Take some printed instructions such as those supplied with a domestic appliance or a game, a cooking recipe, or instructions in a magazine on how to make something, or the instructions on how to fill up a form, and consider whether they are clear and complete or not. If not, determine what is wrong and write some suitable amendments.
2. Draw up a programme of work for yourself for the next two weeks, or longer if you wish. Check each day to see how you progress and record what you actually do in comparison with the programme.
3. Consider a project in which you are involved and draw up a programme of action to complete it. Decide on a suitable method and frequency for monitoring progress and carry this out. Make adequate preparations so that lost progress can be recovered. Make a plan for overcoming any snags that you can foresee. What will you do if unexpected problems arise?
4. How would you test out the following before allowing them to be put into use?
 (a) A lift in a block of flats.
 (b) The staff and the whole system of running a new hotel.
 (c) A new form of examination for school leavers.

(*d*) A tunnel under the Channel.

(*e*) Yourself, if you were to be appointed as chairman of a new company.

5. Describe anything that you are responsible for in terms of a system, making it as large and important as possible. What do you do to control this system and make it continue to function and fulfil its purpose?

6. What are you responsible for the maintenance of? Draw up an appropriate procedure for its maintenance, making improvements on your current practices if possible.

7. Look back over the past week's activities and write down a word or two about what you have achieved. What were your objectives? Are you achieving them? Do you need to modify your objectives, or do you need to alter your own actions or circumstances in some way?

8. The next time you give or receive instructions, make sure that they are repeated back to the person who gives them. Look to see whether any change of opinion is caused by this process.

9. Describe and criticize the way you are supervised by others. Apply the same type of criticism to yourself as a supervisor.

FINALE

16

The Way Ahead

RECAPITULATION

We have now come to the end of the story, having explained
in general what methodical problem-solving is all about and
in detail how it can be done. To recapitulate we may refer to
Figure 14 (p. 252) which shows in graphical form the whole
sequence of stages and steps through which we may pass in
solving a problem methodically. The figure has been drawn
wide in some parts and narrow in others to illustrate, for
example, how the definition of a problem is a narrowing-down
process and how interpretation and the construction of courses
of action are broadening-out processes. Implementation plans
are multi-dimensional because many different actions may
have to be planned out at the same time. The arrowed lines
show the controlling influence of guiding principles and criteria
of preference, and the review of objectives which completes
the cycle.

DEVELOPING INTEREST IN PROBLEM-SOLVING

But now, what are we going to do about it? Where do we go
from here? Making use of a methodical approach is a matter
of learning and commitment, both of which depend very much
on practice. The easy way out if we wished to do nothing
about it would be to say that it is all too simple and obvious

and that we are doing it all the time, or alternatively that it is all wrong. These are excuses to defend laziness or confusion

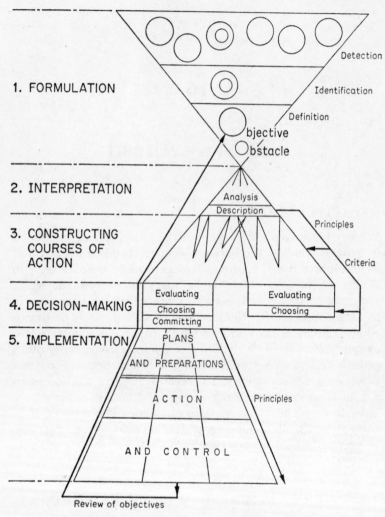

FIGURE 14. The whole problem-solving process

of thought. The fact is that the benefits to be gained from methodical problem-solving are great and they can only be obtained by practice, applying the various methods according to the characteristics of the situations in which we find ourselves.

To adopt a more disciplined form of behaviour requires courage and determination, but once the advantages begin to be appreciated it becomes easier. In due course, as skill develops, the methodical approach becomes 'second nature' and is no longer a formality imposed on our normal ways of dealing with problems. We eventually reach a new level of ability in clear and progressive thinking, in which we know what we are doing at all stages and how to retain control of the situation. If we perceive a difficulty we react quickly and set out to formulate the underlying problem. We identify the objective and the obstacle. If there is time, we plan what is to be done. If the situation is difficult to understand, we analyse it. We develop a strategy and construct courses of action. We evaluate and decide. We plan again, and so on, in a smooth and efficient manner. In the long run we exert control over the flow of problems we face and the level of success we achieve by raising or lowering our objectives.

An admirable way of developing our own personal interest in problem-solving is to work out a system of our own by developing further ways and means of understanding and solving problems. We may draw up a classification of the kinds of problems which interest us and we can work out methods of solving each type, or we can collect examples of useful methods from our own practical experience and from various other sources. Discussing the subject with other people also helps to increase knowledge and interest.

ON MYSTERY

Finally, let me add a word for the reassurance of anyone who may fear that the application of method could take too much of the interest out of life by reducing it to cold logic and system. For this purpose I am going to quote from John Ruskin, the social reformer, art critic, and painter. In a book called *Elements of Drawing* he explained how the components of a landscape painting should be subject to three laws; of 'subordination' to the general laws of nature, such as how trees grow and how mountains and valleys are formed; of 'individuality', whereby all trees and mountains are different and have to be painted so; and of mystery or 'incomprehensibility', whereby it is impossible to know or understand or to paint properly a scene in every minute detail.

'We have, observe, first, Subordination; secondly, Individuality; lastly, and this not the least essential character, Incomprehensibility; a perpetual lesson in every serrated point and shining vein which escape or deceive our sight among the forest leaves, how little we may hope to discern clearly, or judge justly, the rents and veins of the human heart; how much of all that is round us, in men's actions or spirits, which we at first think we understand, a closer and more loving watchfulness would show to be full of mystery, never to be either fathomed or withdrawn.'

Bibliography

A selection of books to read on various aspects of Problem-Solving

DE BONO, E., *The Use of Lateral Thinking* (London: Jonathan Cape, 1967).

DEWEY, J., *How We Think* (London: D. C. Heath and Co., 1909).

DUCKWORTH, E., *A Guide to Operational Research* (London: Methuen University Paperbacks, 1965).

EWING, D. W., *The Human Side of Planning* (London: Collier-Macmillan, 1969).

HAEFELE, J. W., *Creativity and Innovation* (New York: Reinhold Publishing Corporation, 1962. London: Chapman and Hall, 1962).

HAYAKAWA, S. I., *Language in Thought and Action* (London: George Allen and Unwin, 1952).

KEPNER, C. H. and TREGOE, B., *The Rational Manager: A Systematic Approach to Problem Solving and Decision Making* (New York: McGraw-Hill, 1965).

LEE, A. M., *Systems Analysis Frameworks* (London: Macmillan, 1970).

MURRELL, K. F. H., *Ergonomics: Man in his Working Environment* (London: Chapman and Hall, 1965).

PARNES, S. J. and HARDING, H. F., *A Source Book for Creative Thinking* (New York: Charles Scribner and Sons, 1962).

RAYBOULD, E. B. and MINTER, A. L., *Problem Solving for Management* (London: Management Publications Ltd., 1971).

SCHLAIFER, R., *Analysis of Decisions Under Uncertainty* (New York: McGraw-Hill, 1969).

Books referred to in the text

ARGYLE, M., *The Psychology of Interpersonal Behaviour* (Harmondsworth: Penguin Books, 1967).

BACON, F., *Novum Organum and Advancement of Learning*, tr. Devey, J. (London: Bohn, 1864).

CUTLER, A. and McSHANE, R. (tr.), *The Trachtenberg Speed System of Basic Mathematics* (London: Souvenir Press, 1962).

OSBORN, A. F., *Applied Imagination* (New York: Scribner, 1953).

RODGER, A., *The Seven Point Plan* (London: National Institute of Industrial Psychology, 1952).

RUSKIN, J., *Elements of Drawing* (London: George Routledge and Sons, 1857).

SIMBERG, A. L., *Creativity at Work* (Boston: Industrial Education Institute, 1964).

WALLAS, G., *The Art of Thought* (London: Jonathan Cape, 1926).

WHEELER, E., *How to Sell Yourself to Others* (Kingswood: The World's Work, Cedar Books, 1952).

WILSON, E. B., *An Introduction to Scientific Research* (London: McGraw-Hill, 1952).

Report of the Committee of Inquiry on Decimal Currency, Cmnd. 2145 (London: H.M.S.O., 1963).

The First Report of the Royal Commission on Environmental Pollution, Cmnd. 4585 (London: H.M.S.O., 1971).

Index